Thierry Aimar · Francis Bismans
Claude Diebolt

Business Cycles in the Run of History

in collaboration with Reynald Majetti and Zohra Rabah

Springer

Thierry Aimar
BETA/CNRS
Université de Lorraine
Nancy
France

Claude Diebolt
BETA/CNRS
Université de Strasbourg
Strasbourg
France

Francis Bismans
BETA/CNRS
Université de Lorraine
Nancy
France

ISSN 2191-5504 ISSN 2191-5512 (electronic)
SpringerBriefs in Economics
ISBN 978-3-319-24323-8 ISBN 978-3-319-24325-2 (eBook)
DOI 10.1007/978-3-319-24325-2

Library of Congress Control Number: 2015951343

Springer Cham Heidelberg New York Dordrecht London

Printed on acid-free paper

Springer International Publishing AG Switzerland is part of Springer Science+Business Media (www.springer.com)

SpringerBriefs in Economics

More information about this series at http://www.springer.com/series/8876

Contents

Chapter 1
Introduction

Abstract This book is concerned with the development of economic cycles in the run of history. Our main consideration will be the development of cycle theory, with maximum emphasis upon ideas.

Keywords Business cycles · Economics · History

This book deals about business cycles, i.e. economic cycles in the Arthur F. Burns and Wesley C. Mitchell tradition.

A generally accepted definition of business cycles is precisely one presented by Burns and Mitchell in their work *Measuring Business Cycles*. According to Burns and Mitchell:

> Business cycles are a type of fluctuation found in the aggregate economic activity of nations to organize their work mainly in business enterprises: a cycle consists of expansions occurring at about the same time in many economic activities, followed by similarly general recessions, contractions, and revivals which merge into the expansion phase of the next cycle; this sequence of changes is recurrent but not periodic; in duration business cycles vary from more than one year to ten or twelve years; they are not divisible into shorter cycles with amplitudes approximating their own. (Burns and Mitchell 1946, p. 3).

The definition of business cycles advanced by Burns and Mitchell emphasizes that cycles are *recurrent but not periodic*. For some, the term *business cycles* implies a certain rhythm of business activity. To describe the cycle as recurrent means that it possesses a repetitive pattern of development—a pattern of expansion, recession, contraction, and revival, followed by renewed expansion. The cycle, however, is uniform neither in time periods nor in amplitude. We cannot say that the expansion phase always lasts X months and measures of aggregate activity rise Y per cent above the preceding low point. There is a high degree of uniformity from one cycle to the next in the forces of cumulation. Upswings and downswings

T. Aimar et al., *Business Cycles in the Run of History*,
SpringerBriefs in Economics, DOI 10.1007/978-3-319-24325-2_1

are self-reinforcing; they feed on themselves, possess similar characteristics, and show approximately concurrent movements in many different series. However, there is no evidence that they recur again and again in virtually the same form and amplitude. The completion of a cycle from trough to trough or peak to peak may take from approximately two to more than ten years, and the proportions of the upswing and downswing may vary all the way from mild to catastrophic.

Let us now turn to a consideration of the four phases of the business cycle—expansion, recession, contraction, and revival—and attempt to summarize the salient features of each phase. It is well to remember that this description is one of possible features found only in a composite view of all cycles. Features found in an individual cyclical experience may differ in some measure from the generalizations that follow.

The features typical of expansion are a large volume of production and trade; a high level of employment and job opportunities in sufficient abundance to permit a good deal of labor mobility; rising commodity prices; a rising structure of interest rates; advancing prices of equity securities; a growing volume of borrowings at both the business and consumer level; and a substantial volume of investment in machinery, alterations in plant, and additions to capacity by business.

The essence of expansion is the way in which each of these developments reinforces the others. There is a snowballing effect. As trade and production expand, the demand for labor is thereby stimulated, and hours of work are lengthened. Increased employment in its turn leads to larger wage payments that extend the market for consumers' goods and so further stimulate trade and production. The expansion in demand brings increases in the prices of finished goods, of the materials used in their processing, and of services provided for business and consumers. Favorable profit prospects growing out of the general expansion in trade and production give, in their own turn, a further stimulus, thus promoting a still further increase in employment and new advances in prices. Economic opportunities seem to exist in abundance, and the problem for most firms is likely to be squeezing the maximum output from existing facilities. Investment in capital facilities is encouraged, which gives renewed impetus to the demand for goods and services, to employment, to income receipts, to price level, and to production and trade. This advance may in turn improve profit prospects, maintain optimism, and so stimulate investment outlays once again.

Yet factors emerge during the expansion phase, which limit its extent and duration. Stresses appear which, though they may be temporarily overcome, reappear, seemingly with renewed vigor. Business weaknesses accumulate toward the latter part of the expansion phase. These weaknesses are eventually reflected in a squeeze on business profits. Unit costs of output rise with the increasing price of raw materials and with the tendency of wage rates to outstrip the advance in labor productivity because of the breaking in of new and less efficient employees and the use of substandard equipment in order to achieve capacity output; the increased demand for credit raises the interest cost to borrowers; the rush to maximize production to meet market demand means the business expanses tend to be scrutinized less closely.

So long as higher costs can be passed along to consumers in the form of higher prices, profit margins are little affected. However, it becomes increasingly difficult to adopt this remedy universally. In some industries the optimism of the expansion phase has probably found expression in expansion of capacity somewhat in excess of current market needs and whatever accretions in demand that will take place in the immediate future. New equipment and facilities add greatly to the supply of goods increases, and it becomes difficult to raise selling prices further. Profits are caught between advancing costs and a level of prices that is under growing competitive pressure. Less satisfactory profits are likely to force a reassessment of market prospects and to influence adversely the climate of business opinion, curtailing the spending plans of business. Reduced spending by business is reflected in reduced employment opportunities, less overtime, probable layoffs, and smaller income disbursements. Accompanying these developments may be a desire to liquidate inventories to bring their level more into line with new and less buoyant prospects for sales. Related industries may now be forced to similarly revise their spending and scheduling plans, as will those consuming units dependent for their incomes upon their areas of production. These developments, in their turn, influence retail spending.

Accompanying the new situation in production and trade are changed conditions in the money and credit markets. During the early phases of expansion, bank loans expand in unison with the growth in bank deposits. However, in the latter stages banks become *loaned up*, that is, the ration of loans to deposits approaches a level beyond which it is not safe to go lest liquidity be unduly impaired. Interest rates rise, and more exacting standards for new loans and for renewals are set. A higher structure of interest rates prevails throughout the money market. Higher loan rates and greater difficulties in obtaining credit place yet other restrictions upon the ability of enterprises to continue expanding.

Even though some incomes are unaffected by the changing business prospects, total income disbursements fall. Those whose incomes are maintained may attempt to consolidate and make their financial positions more liquid. Consuming and business units which may have taken on debts during the expansion phase deem it unwise to add to their indebtedness in the face of less favorable prospects. Their emphasis is upon debt reduction; and major outlays, for which new financing might be necessary, are postponed.

The feature of contraction is the reverse of those of expansion. The volume of production and trade shrinks, employment declines, and unemployment rises; job opportunities diminish; commodity prices fall; the structure of interest rates falls, and the prices of high-grade bonds rise; the prices of equity securities decline; the demand for borrowings on the part of both business and the consumer is reduced; there are retrenchments in capital outlays, particularly in business spending on machinery, equipment, and plant additions. Optimism gives way to pessimism. These developments accumulate and reinforce themselves. Declining production and a reduced volume of trade curtail the demand for labor. Overtime is eliminated, and employment reduced. Pay envelopes are smaller and fewer, with the consequent unfavorable effect upon retail trade, thus further depressing production. Reduced demand brings reductions in the price of raw materials and in wholesale prices. Prices of retail goods and of services are likely to be more sluggish in their decline. Wage rates and long-term interest rates also respond rather slowly. The fall in expenses lags behind the fall in revenues, and this squeezes profits further; many firms show losses. Pessimism becomes widespread and leads to further retrenchment in the spending plans of business and consuming units.

The burdens of contraction are not shared equally by all segments of the economy. Consumer demand for durable goods is more affected than that for non-durable. Durable goods are particularly sensitive to lower wage disbursements and poorer earnings prospects. In the face of falling demand businessmen increase their efforts to liquidate stocks and reduce their inventory-sales rations. The inventory accumulation of expansion turns to liquidation in contraction. Especially affected is business spending for plant and equipment. New orders for equipment sink, for incentive to add to capacity or to replace equipment is nonexistent when operating levels are low and industry is generally burdened with over-capacity. Inventory liquidation and a reduced volume of production and trade diminish demand by business for working capital and for long-term credit. Bank loans fall, and there is increased competition among long-term lenders and banks to place funds. The structure of interest rates declines as the demand for high-grade debt instruments grows.

In contraction as in expansion all forces seem to be operating in one direction. One shrinkage forces others and through the stream of spending comes back to react upon itself. Yet, in contraction as in expansion, relations change and accumulate to bring about a reversal in the direction of the aggregate. Often, one of the first points of reversal is in the market for equities. The decline in security prices lowers the price-earnings ratio so that equities once again become attractive and arouse renewed investor interest. Within business firms adjustments are made to improve profit margins. Expenses are brought into line, wastes are eliminated, and efficiency is emphasized. Reorganization may serve to reduce overheads costs, and operating expenses in manufacturing firms are reduced by lower costs of raw materials and employment of only the most experienced workers.

The lower level of interest rates, "cheap money", means that both short-term credit and long-term financing can be had on very favorable terms. Further, manufacturing and trading firms may have allowed inventories to reach minimum levels; to reduce them further would be to run the risk of losing sales. Goods sold from a minimum stock level require replacement, and new orders ensue. Demand for replacement may be forthcoming from both consumers and business firms. Many family units will be called upon to replace goods no longer serviceable. Some purchases can no longer be postponed. Favorable installment credit terms are available and can provide another impetus to production and trade. Industry will possibly be faced with the need of replacing equipment or plant that has become technologically obsolescent or for which further repair is uneconomical. To the extent that such orders are forthcoming, demand is stimulated.

Business and consumer demand may receive further impetus from the knowledge that prices have fallen during contraction and that there are limits to the extent of the decline. Purchases can be made at bargain rates, and there is little advantage in delaying longer.

These encouraging signs become more and more numerous. They break a wall of pessimism, and gradually a measured optimism emerges. Tangible improvements in particular industries arising from increased spending by businesses and consumers augment the more encouraging circumstances. Revival is under way, and it gathers momentum as expansion in particular areas spreads to related segments of business activity. It may be speeded by any favorable development, such as an increase in foreign buying, the enthusiastic acceptance of new-model automobile, or the introduction of a major cutting technique affecting many areas of business. Conversely, revival may be checked or slowed by unfavorable developments from outside the business system. Be that as it may, there is a snowballing which sooner or later will lead aggregate activity once again into the expansion phase.

In view of this, the present book is concerned with the development of economic cycles in the run of history. In a short essay like this, it is of course impossible to treat fully all the theories or to mention all those who have contributed to the literature. Therefore, our main consideration will be the development of cycle theory, with maximum emphasis upon ideas. Chapter 2 delivers an overview of the debate about cycles before the 1970s. Chapter 3 completes this survey by presenting the main empirical investigations since that time. Finally, Chaps. 4 and 5 illustrate the discourse, by presenting, in the tradition of Burns and Mitchell, original case studies on France and South Africa, and Germany. An afterword concludes in Chap. 6.

Reference

Burns, A. F., & Mitchell, W. C. (1946). *Measuring business cycles*. New York: National Bureau of Economic Research.

Chapter 2
Theory

Abstract Technical progress and economic growth occur mainly in cycles of efforts and tensions, with breaks of various scales and intensity. Economic history shows how relativistic these movements are: they are not necessarily to be found in all economic systems nor in all countries. Some characterise a period, others an economy. Hence the nature of each cycle depends on the socio-economic systems which generate it, although their causes and periodicities might vary through history, depending on the economic structures of the countries in question. However, without a theory or a combination of theories, the study of economic cycles is both impractical and sterile.

Keywords Business cycles · Cliometrics · Economics · Economic growth · Economic history · History · History of economic thought · Methodology

Technical progress and economic growth occur mainly in cycles of efforts and tensions, with breaks of various scales and intensity. Economic history shows how relativistic these movements are: they are not necessarily to be found in all economic systems nor in all countries. Some characterise a period, others an economy. In fact each cycle derives part of its specifics from a more fundamental underlying movement. Hence the nature of each cycle depends on the socio-economic systems which generate it, although their causes and periodicities might vary through history, depending on the economic structures of the countries in question.

However, without a theory or a combination of theories, the study of economic cycles is both impractical and sterile. Obviously there is no need to endorse the fundamental causes identified by one theory or another but it is necessary to understand the effects these causes have on economic life as well as the repercussions of the various elements on one another.

T. Aimar et al., *Business Cycles in the Run of History*,
SpringerBriefs in Economics, DOI 10.1007/978-3-319-24325-2_2

In this chapter, we do not aim to repeat the comprehensive work of the great economists of the past such as Haberler (1937) or Schumpeter (1939, 1954). We will start with a selection of results which we consider as accepted, which come from various studies' experience-based conclusions and their confrontation with economists' essential hypotheses, investigating causes and analysing the economic cycle, to contribute some additional elements to the most recent theoretical, statistical and econometric developments.

In line with our statement on the relativity of economic fluctuations, we should specify that we do not again mean here to discuss in extenso Schumpeter's distinction (1939) between cycles of the Kitchen, Juglar and Kondratieff types, with their respective periodicities. We will mainly deal with the shorter cycle, which can also be called the "classical" cycle.

2.1 The "Old Decennial Cycle" and Its Theorizations

Economic fluctuations existed already before the Industrial Revolution and in many cases they could be explained by the alternation of good and bad harvests. However, no regular pattern could be observed in this alternation, as exogenous events obviously came to blur the graph of a possible endogenous rhythm, inherent in the very nature of economic dynamics.

2.1.1 Industrial Crises

During the 19th century, fluctuations were more frequent and more regular. At the same time, the harvests had a lower impact, both because of the growing importance of manufacturing industries and because the opening up of the world market made it possible to compensate for the shortage of agricultural products. Moreover, the importance of technical and particularly financial factors increased. Crises had a tendency to become industrial. One of their main characteristics was that they were affected by a general overproduction. Ricardo (1821, ed. Sraffa, p. 265), when he published the first edition of his *Principles* in 1817, had the example of the English crisis of 1815 right under his nose and he made sure he stressed the phenomenon: "The commencement (…) of peace after a long war, generally produces considerable distress in Trade. It changes in a great degree the nature of the employments to which the respective of countries were before devoted;; and during the interval while they are settling in the situations which new circumstances have made the most beneficial, much fixed capital is unemployed, perhaps wholly lost, and labourers are without full employment".

The 1815 crisis, which was followed by another one in 1818–1819, was to raise fierce controversies about possible general overproduction and Say's law, between

Sismondi (1827) and Malthus (1820) on the one hand and Ricardo (1821) and Say (1815–1821) on the other.

However, economic historians, such as Bairoch (1997, pp. 401–402) generally agree to date the first real "modern" crisis back to 1825. According to Hicks' interpretation (1989, Chap. 11; also 1981), this first crisis was followed by others in 1836–1837 (which hit mainly the United States), 1848, 1857 and 1867; later the phenomenon weakened, at least in Great Britain. When one looks at this succession of dates, the notion of cycle comes immediately to mind as these crises seemed to happen at 10-year periodicities. This is the "classical cycle", the "old" cycle to use the terminology of Hicks (1989).

Two authors, Stuart Mill (1848, book III, Chap. 12) and Marx (1894, book III, Sect. 5), although they did not have much experience of crises, produced a good analysis of this classical cycle and particularly of its critical point, namely the crisis. For the two of them, the explanation focused on England and stressed the influence of credit mechanisms as well as the role of the Bank of England. For Marx (1894, book III, volume 7, p. 151): "(...) the whole crisis seems to be merely a credit and money crisis"; for Stuart Mill (1848, p. 528): "the fall, as well as the rise, originating not anything affecting money, but in the state of credit".

Here in fact is the underlying explanatory scheme of these two authors. In the early days of economic depression, prices and interest rates were low compared to the values observed during the prosperous period. Progressively, the recovery of economic activity induced a rise in some prices, while the interest rates remained low. The financing of an increasing price level was rather unproblematic, using bills of exchange. However there came a time when trade credit was not sufficient anymore; firms turned then to bank credit, which meant that bank rates were pushed up. In the long run, the accumulation of bills of exchange in the banks' portfolios, as well as speculation encouraged by a lasting price increase, resulted in a mistrust of bank notes. This distrust resulted in a sudden increase of the basic currency, i.e. gold. Second-rank banks which did not have sufficient reserves to face the demand for gold would turn towards the Bank of England, which, when its metal reserves started to dwindle, made credit more expensive and in so doing plunged the economy in a crisis.

Hence it was the Bank of England which triggered the crisis and the resulting bankruptcies of banks and firms as well as the fall in prices when it tried to protect its gold reserves. To curb the further collapse of prices and put the economy back on the road to prosperity, the Bank of England had to restore the banks' and firms' confidence by lowering its bank rate at the appropriate time. This is what Hicks called Thornton's precept (Bagehot's lender of last resort comes immediately to mind, but in fact Thornton came much earlier as his *Paper Credit* dates back to 1802!).

Actually the Bank of England was to make this concept its own progressively and to learn to handle its bank rate wisely. It thus acquired the means to avoid major crises so that in the 1860s, cyclical fluctuations became less marked, at least in Great Britain.

2.1.2 Classical Business Cycles

Nevertheless the long series of quasi-decennial cycles which started in 1825 was bound to raise questions among economists. Two of them, William Stanley Jevons and Clément Juglar, decided to look into the issue. In some ways they followed similar approaches, especially as they were much more interested in cycles than in crises: this was a major break with their predecessors. Furthermore they made extensive use of the available time series. However, they differed on two main points: the strict periodicity of the fluctuations and the analysis of their causes.

Jevons really started to do research on cycles in the 1870s, after he had already a solid reputation as a theoretician, in particular with the publication in 1871 of his *Theory of Political Economy*, which ranked him—together with Walras and Menger—among the initiators of marginalism. In a 1875 writing (1884, pp. 194–205), he first formulated the hypothesis that sunspot cycles (of a duration of 11.1 years) implied a temperature cycle which in turn caused a harvest cycle and in fine a cycle of grain prices. It was however difficult for Jevons to connect the periodicity of sunspots with that of grain prices, a series which did not provide identifiable variations. He therefore turned to the analysis of credit cycles between 1825 and 1867, which, according to him, presented a periodicity of 10.8 years. There remained a gap between both durations which Jevons was unable to explain. In the end, in his publication *The Periodicity of Commercial Crises and its Physical Explanation* written in 1878—Jevons (1884, pp. 206–220)—he concluded, on the basis of new calculations, that there was a credit cycle which had an average length of between 10.3 and 10.46 years. Since a new study of sunspots made it possible to date the periodicity of the corresponding cycle to 10.45 years, Jevons (1884, p. 215) was in a position to assert that "it becomes highly probable that the two periodic phenomena (…) are connected as cause and effect".

Juglar, whose book *Commercial Crises* was first published in 1862 with a second edition in 1889, studied the course of crises in France, England and the United States. Schumpeter (1954) considered him as "one of the greatest economists of all times". His method was comparative and was based on the empirical study of long series. In short, his approach was supposed to be scientific: "if we rely not only on statistical data, but also on large numbers, long periods in three big countries, we consider that we have met the main conditions of a scientific demonstration better than arguable assertions." (1862, p. XII).

For Juglar, there was almost no doubt about the fundamental cause of crises and hence of cycles: once accidental causes or specific events had been discarded, the cause of crises was to be found in the modifications of credit conditions, especially the development of discounts and he therefore assumed that the evolution of currency flows played a major role.

It should be mentioned that in his second edition (1889), Juglar's approach remained identical, but at the same time he specified that he used more numerous statistical data and he considered a longer period of time. Moreover he differentiated himself from Jevons by refusing any strict periodicity of the cycle and he just noted that crises occurred "over a period of 5 to 10 years". In this second edition, Juglar also proposed an analysis of the cycle phases, which is still used today: prosperity duration of 5 to 7 years, crisis duration from a few months to some years; depression duration some years.

2.2 The Years of High Theory

The Great Depression of the 1930s was without precedent, utterly different from the 19th century classical crises in both form and scale, and was to produce abundant theoretical literature. Out of this crop, well analysed by Haberler (1937), in spite of his close proximity to these debates, two names emerged: Hayek, the best-known representative of the Austrian economics school, and Keynes.

2.2.1 Austrian Theory

The Austrian theory of the business cycle fits into a more general context of economic literature's between-the-wars interest in questions of economic conjuncture, which was accentuated by the 1929 crash. From a different angle, the theory is linked to a traditional subject for the Austrians, the mode of integration of money to real phenomena. Although theirs is not the only work in the Austrian theory of the cycle, Mises and Hayek are its two main authors.

Mises initiated a theoretical representation of the channels of influence of money on the real economy in *The Theory of Money and Credit* (1912); it explains economic disturbances as the effects of money creation on the relative prices structure. He developed this analysis between the wars (see the section of *Money, Method and the Market Process* (1990) on monetary questions (pp. 55–109)) and *Human Action* (1966).

Hayek's first economic research was on trade cycle theory in the middle of the 1920s. Following a research trip to the USA (1923–1924), he wrote several articles on the problems of fluctuations in the market economy (1925–1929), the most important of which were translated into English and were published in a 1985 collection, together with later texts, entitled *Money, Capital and Fluctuations, Early Essays*. Hayek's first full length book, in a similar vein, was entitled *Monetary Theory and Trade Cycle* (1928b). He especially developed his ideas during a cycle of four conferences at the London School of Economics, on Lionel Robbins' invitation. They were immediately published under the title *Prices and Production* (1931). This is undoubtedly at the very centre of Hayek's theories—and the most stylistic—on the subject. It unleashed a barrage of arguments from such illustrious figures as Keynes, Sraffa and Hicks; but even today is the work of reference on Austrian cycle analysis.

Prices and Production stressed the issue of agents' success in their expectations, or in other words, coordination of their plans. Hayek thus concentrates his analysis of modes of interaction between the producers/entrepreneurs and the employees in the shape of consumers/savers, studying procedures of finding compatibility and adjustment between the producer/entrepreneurs' plans and the employees' inter-temporal consumer choices. Coordination requires consumers' plans and producers' strategies to be mutually compatible so that the saved part of consumers' incomes will equal the volume of investments generated by firms. Conversely, crisis is described in theoretical terms as the expression of generalized discoordination between, firstly, entrepreneurs' choices in factor allocation for producing consumer and investment goods and secondly, employees' preferences in directing income to consumption or saving.

The theory presents a trilogy between interest rates, relative prices and capital seen as a structural, heterogeneous whole. Money plays a sustained, central role. The distribution of credit initiates the cycle—with an expansion phase—and ends it by producing depression. The creation of liquid assets separates technical processes from subjective choices: it makes the organisation of the production structure incoherent with regard to agents' inter-temporal preferences in terms of orientation of resources.

Sudden adjustments by quantity occurs when credit distribution and its consequence, raised income, dissipates monetary illusion and empowers consumers to once again make their point of view heard when production choices are being made. However, the inevitable move from boom to bust is based on a concept of the rapport between reality and the monetary; it requires the thorough application of a strict timetable.

Hayek does not try to determine a relation between the general price level and an aggregate production level. He studies the consequences of monetary expansion on the distribution of resources between the sectors of investment goods and consumption goods. For him, money enters the real system at specific points, in a sequential way, and has an impact on the structure of production through the interest rate. This relation between capital and interest is one of the characteristics of the Austrian approach. The fall of the monetary interest rate below the natural rate (or equilibrium rate, reflecting the inter-temporal preferences of the wage-earners-consumers) starts the cycle. Considering the strong sensitivity to interest rates of the relatively more capitalised sectors upstream of the production structure, investment there is artificially stimulated ("mal-investment").

The Austrian theory of cycles tells a story of linked distortions; distortion between the equilibrium rate and the monetary rate, distortion of investment within the production structure, distortion of the relative prices between investment goods and consumption goods, distortion between monetary credit supply and real savings supply. But in the development of the Austrian cycle, chronology is of major importance. The dialectics of money and capital, governed by the game of relative prices, is organised around certain time-lines, characterised by the notions of sequence, lag and, above all, rigidity. The expansion of credit leads to time bugging, not only because its produces false information (money illusion) but also by encouraging specific forms of rigidity: rigidity of interest, as during the boom phase the pursuit of monetary expansion prevents the money rate from reaching the rate balance; price rigidity, for if errors are made and it takes time to correct them, this is due to prices not adapting immediately to the subjective data and not performing their informative and predictive function[1]; rigidity of inter-temporal agent-preferences, considered as given and constant from the beginning to the end of the cycle. If agents were to change their inter-temporal consumption choices during the period of analysis, the second phase of the cycle, the crisis, would not occur.

2.2.2 The Keynesian Revolution

Keynes' *General Theory* (1936) is of course not devoted to studying or explaining the cycle. However, Chap. 22 provides a precise idea of the problematic raised by the author. The analysis uses the complete set of Keynesian conceptual tools: propensity to consume, the multiplier effect, the principle of effective demand, liquidity preference and above all the marginal efficiency of capital. For Keynes (1936, pp. 313–311), the latter is the main explanatory factor of trade cycles. We should recall here that for a given type of capital good, marginal efficiency is defined as "that rate of discount which would make the present value of the series of annuities given by the returns expected from the capital-asset during its life just equal to its supply price" (Keynes 1936, p. 135). The supply price of a capital good could also be called its "replacement cost", i.e. the fair price high enough to incite the manufacturer to produce an additional unit of this good. This price is determined during the current period. This does not apply to expected returns which by definition are calculated by taking the near and distant future into account. The new investment results from a comparison between global marginal efficiency and the actual interest rate; it takes place only if the former is higher than the latter.

One point should be made about the "subject" who calculates the expected efficiency of various types of capital. This subject does not actually exist, according to Keynes; it is in fact the stock exchanges which assess (and re-assess) daily the value of most investments. To use the *General Theory*'s words (1936, p. 151), "certain classes of investment are governed by the average expectation of those who deal on the Stock Exchange as revealed in the price of shares, rather by the

[1]Hicks noted: "When the market rate is reduced below the natural rate, what will happen to the quantities of inputs and outputs? The correct answer, on these assumptions, is very simple: the effect will be nil. Prices will rise uniformly; and that is that. When the Wicksell model is taken strictly (as it was being taken strictly), it is in Neutral equilibrium … Thus there is no room for a prolonged discrepancy between market rate and natural rate if there is instantaneous adjustment of prices. Money prices will simply rise uniformly; and that is that" (Hicks 1967, p. 206). Hicks (1967, p. 206).

genuine expectations of the professional entrepreneur". It should be added that this average expectation relies on a pure convention, the essence of which is to assume that the present state of affairs will continue indefinitely unless there are very good reasons to expect a change. Keynes states that such a conventional assessment basis is "the outcome of the mass psychology of a large number of ignorant individuals". But the essential task of professionals and speculators active on the financial markets is to anticipate modifications of the conventional assessment basis before the general public does. Consequently these markets function in a rather hectic way and with great volatility, as they are subject to unreasonable waves of optimism and pessimism.

All this said, let us turn now to Keynes' explanations of economic cycles and consider the question from the viewpoint of the economic boom's last stages. As is well known, the interest rate is in upward trend as a consequence of an increased demand for money to meet both commercial and speculative needs. This is not, however, the main point: what actually characterises the end of the boom is the traders' expectations and their estimations of the stock market yields being so optimistic that they neglect the increasing production costs and the increasing interest rates which characterise this phase of the cycle. The crisis then coincides with a sudden collapse of the marginal efficiency of capital. It is easy to explain why this reversal has to be large scale and brutal, since financial markets, as noted by Keynes (1936, p. 316), are under the double influence "…of purchasers largely ignorant of what they are buying and of speculators who are more concerned with forecasting the next shift of market sentiment than with a reasonable estimate of the future yield of capital-assets". Uncertainty about the future and the collapse of the marginal efficiency of capital leads to an increase of the preference for liquidity and hence a new rise of the interest rate, which in turn further damages confidence levels. The drop of the interest rate would certainly later constitute a prerequisite to economic recovery during the recession phase but once the crisis has started, the drop in marginal efficiency continues and is sustained.

Time is therefore needed (three to five years according to Keynes) before trust is restored and marginal efficiency of capital recovers, a period during which the decrease in interest rates may—in extreme cases—even prove insufficient to revive an anaemic marginal efficiency. All the more time to recover is needed as the collapse of marginal efficiency has a negative impact on the propensity to consume, through the simultaneous collapse of stock markets and of speculators' income. Demand as a whole falls off.

The recession only really ends when capital marginal efficiency curves upwards once again, a phenomenon objectively linked to the fact that capital has become sufficiently rare; a best left new cycle can then begin.

It is to Keynes to conclude this analysis (1936, p. 320), "…in conditions of *laissez-faire* the avoidance of wide fluctuations in employment may, therefore, prove impossible without a far-reaching change in the psychology of investment markets such as there is no reason to expect. I conclude that the duty of ordering the current volume of investment cannot safely be left in private hands."

2.3 Keynesianism and Around

Keynes' analysis of the cycle was in line with the public works policies of the 1930s, the New Deal etc., all of which were attempts to get out of the Great Depression by stimulating effective global demand. As for Hayek's theory of economic fluctuations, it was much less in line. Lawrence R. Klein's appreciation—a future Nobel Prize laureate—clearly explains this difference: (1949, p. 52) "Hayek's description of the economic process just does not fit the facts". It is therefore not surprising that the economists who were studying the cycle turned to Keynes' theory and that Hayek's analyses comparatively disappeared from the public eye for a long while.

2.3.1 The Keynesian School

Applying Keynesian policies to support economic activity was to prove very efficient, as the period of the Thirty Glorious Years did not experience any significant general recession. Full employment seemed to have become a permanent state of the economy. Moreover, as noted by Hicks (1981, p. 344), the few recessions which occurred in some specific countries, resulted most of the time from "political pressure".

These *post festum* findings were anticipated by Kalecki (1943b) who talked of a "political business cycle" which would substitute the traditional cycle. His main argument is that it is technically impossible for the State to bring the economy to the point of full employment and to maintain it there. Industrial leaders in fact opposed such a level since "their class instinct tells them that lasting full employment is unsound from their point of view". And Kalecki therefore devised the typical political cycle[2]: during recessions, under the pressure of the workers, governments used to increase public investment based on loan in order to avoid mass unemployment. The consequence was economic recovery which led to full employment. Should public authorities use the same "Keynesian" techniques to maintain a high employment level, the pressure and opposition from the business circles would become so strong that they would lead governments to revert to budgetary orthodoxy. As a result, recession would be back and would require new state intervention, etc.

Moreover, the Cambridge economist's conceptual system, as soon as the *General Theory* was published, was taken up and developed by several authors. Alvin Hansen's book published in 1941 is important not so much on the theoretical level as on the economic policy level: it is a true manifesto in favour of a Keynesian full employment policy. It is therefore not surprising that Hansen's

[2]Later on the meaning of the term "political cycle" evolved and was used for a purely electoral cycle: see for instance Nordhaus (1975).

objective (1941, p. 292) was for instance "to minimize the cycle movement by a system of fluctuating tax rates." Generally speaking, he favoured a budget policy as a means to compensate for the impact on employment of private investment variations, as well as to ensure the boosting of the economy: this is the "pump-priming".

However, several authors, often young ones, will try to think the cycle anew basing their theorizations on the foundations of *General Theory*. The first one to do so was R.F. Harrod, who published his *Trade Cycle* in 1936. Harrod (1936, p. 102) considered that the cycle could be explained by the interactions between the Multiplier and the "Relation" (author's capitals). By "Relation", he meant nothing else but the acceleration principle, i.e. the influence of spending or income variations on investments. This principle as such was nothing new as one can date back its origins to Aftalion (1913), or even Marx. It gave rise to numerous discussions after World War I: J.M. Clark, A. Spiethoff, S. Kuznets, A.C. Pigou, W.C. Mitchell, D.H. Robertson are some of the names which come to mind in that respect. What was new with the author of *Trade Cycle*, is on the one hand his really dynamic concept of the effects of acceleration and on the other the study of interconnections between the multiplier and the accelerator: Harrod (1936, p. 70) even claimed that with this study he had "revealed the secret of the trade cycle". It should be noted however that although Harrod really dynamized the acceleration effect, like Keynes he continued to conceive the multiplier as an instantaneous—hence static—relation between investment and income.

The second author was the Polish economist, Michal Kalecki. Strictly speaking, Kalecki (1936) was not Keynesian, as evidenced by his criticism of the *General Theory*. However, if he criticized Keynes for not properly modeled investment demand, he acknowledged that he had exhaustively analyzed the relationship between the variations in investment and the general movement of production and employment. Indeed, independently of Keynes, Kalecki (1935a, b, 1943a, 1954) developed a model with a remarkably stable nucleus even if it gave rise to different kinds of interpretations. We will focus here on one single interpretation, that given in 1935. We will however modify Kalecki's notations and we will neither take up his assumption that workers' savings were non-existent nor his distinction between capitalists and workers.

Kalecki reasoned within a closed economy, in which the income or product could be split into consumption C, investment (net expenditure) I and autonomous expenditure A. Since A is constant and $C = cY$, income is determined, via the instantaneous multiplier, by

$$Y(t) = (I(t) + A)/(1 - c). \tag{2.1}$$

Orders of equipment goods at time t, denoted by B, generate corresponding deliveries and finally investment outlays $I(t)$, defined net of replacement, after a fixed lag θ. In mean, we have:

$$I(t) = \frac{1}{\theta} \int_{t-\theta}^{t} B(t)dt. \tag{2.2}$$

Denote by $K(t)$ the capital stock at the instant t. Its derivative with respect to time $K'(t)$ is the rate of deliveries of new capital goods, so that

$$\frac{d}{dt}K(t) = B(t-\theta). \tag{2.3}$$

By assumption $B(t)$ is positively related to the saving rate and negatively to the current capital stock[3]:

$$B(t) = a(1-c)Y(t) - kK(t), \quad a, k > 0. \tag{2.4}$$

The relations (2.1), (2.2), (2.3) and (2.4) form a system of four equations with four unknowns: $Y(t)$, $I(t)$, $K(t)$ and $B(t)$. After some substitutions, we obtain a mixed difference-differential equation:

$$\frac{dK(t)}{dt} = \frac{a}{\theta}K(t) - \left(k + \frac{a}{\theta}\right)K(t-\theta). \tag{2.5}$$

The mathematical treatment of Eq. (2.5) has been given by Frisch and Holme (1935). It yields the following conclusions: the model admits as unique solution a sinusoidal function; the period of oscillation is several times the length of the lag θ; the oscillations may be regular or damped according to the values of coefficients a and k.

2.3.2 The Samuelson-Hicks Model

Samuelson (1939), although he would not acknowledge it, was totally in keeping with the Harrodian analysis.[4] His contribution was twofold: on the one hand he explicitly included governmental expenses in global demand; on the other he developed a dynamic cycle model which can be expressed in three equations:

$$\begin{cases} Y_t = C_t + I_t + G_t \\ C_t = \alpha Y_{t-1} \\ I_t = \beta(C_t - C_{t-1}). \end{cases} \tag{2.6}$$

The notations are explicit enough; hence we will only specify that I represents exclusively private investment, α the marginal propensity to spend and β the acceleration coefficient.

[3]One could insert an additional variable in function (2.6) which would represent a trend, possibly a variable trend in the long run.

[4]Samuelson (1939) claimed the merit for the study of multiplier-accelerator interactions was all Hansen's, who was also his PhD supervisor. A quick reading of Samuelson's article shows the obvious influence of Harrod, although Samuelson mentioned it not once. For instance he used repeatedly the typically "Harrodian" term "relation" to name the acceleration principle.

If we assume that governmental expenditure G is exogenous to the model, we have the difference equation of second order

$$Y_t = G_0 + \alpha(1+\beta)Y_{t-1} - \alpha\beta Y_{t-2}. \tag{2.7}$$

The solution to (2.7)—which remains simple since its coefficients are constant and there are only two lags to take into consideration—depends on the roots of the characteristic equation $x^2 + \alpha(1+\beta)x + \alpha\beta = 0$, themselves functions of the parameters α and β. The set of possible values of α et β is divided into four areas, each of which gives different sample paths for the national revenue[5]: in synthesis, there are cyclical fluctuations (damped, regular or explosive) when the roots of characteristic equation are complex conjugate numbers, i.e. when $\alpha < (4\beta/(1+\beta)^2)$. In other terms, national revenue swings temporally if the marginal propensity to consume is weak and the acceleration coefficient is large or vice versa.

Samuelson's model makes it possible, under specific circumstances, to create fluctuations which differ from real cycles from three points of view: (1) the oscillations of the model are regular only in a very specific case, i.e. when the marginal propensity to spend equals the reversed coefficient of acceleration; (2) as opposed to the observed cycles, these oscillations are perfectly symmetrical; (3) their magnitude depends on the initial conditions of the model whereas, the magnitude of real cycles varies and should at least be explained. (Samuelson's model was long-lasting; we should note Selten and Guth's (1982) contribution to it, their originality being to introduce Nash's bargaining solution in the frame of a simple multiplier-accelerator model.)

In 1950 Hicks took up again the issue of the oscillator to which he added his personal touch, so that soon one started talking about the 'Samuelson-Hicks model". However, although Hicks (1950, p. 83) considered the case where the model experienced explosive oscillations, the Oxford economist modified Samuelson's analysis on three major points:

1. He substituted the framework of a "progressive" economy—and hence growth at a constant rate—for that of a stable economy.
2. He introduced a cyclical ceiling in that at each period, the national income could go beyond a certain level defined by full employment of production factors.
3. Finally he introduced also a cyclical floor which limited the downward variations of revenue; the existence of such a floor is plausible since the disinvestment following this drop is at any time necessarily limited by the tempo of throwing out equipment; in other words, the accelerator stops releasing these effects from the moment the floor is reached.

All in all, Hicks provided an overview of economic dynamics which showed that economies experiencing a cyclical growth movement and fluctuations were

[5]For a comprehensive analysis of the model and its solutions, see Chiang et al. (2005, pp. 578 sq).

constrained by the full employment ceiling and the very progressive disuse of capital goods. As such his model is much closer to real life than the simple multiplier-accelerator model.

2.3.3 "Non-linear" Contributions of Goodwin and Allais

Samuelson's and Hicks' approaches are based formally on linear equations systems; however, it is possible to introduce nonlinearities in the analysis while keeping the same conceptual framework. One of the first to explore this path was Nicholas Kaldor. In fact, he supposed that the values of the marginal propensity to consume and the accelerator were not stable but varied with the production level. It was therefore possible to generate a cycle endogenously—Kaldor (1940, especially pp. 89–92)—so that the magnitude of the fluctuations would not depend on the initial conditions or random shocks.

The method used by Kaldor was mainly graphic. This was not true of the two other economists who both constructed a true mathematical model, namely Goodwin and Allais.

Goodwin (1951) has developed a model which combines dynamic multiplier and non-linear accelerator. As in Kalecki, there is a fixed-time delay θ in the accelerator; then θ is an average lag between investment decisions and outlays, i.e. $I(t) = B(t - \theta)$. The accelerator is defined as a relation between total outlays $B(t)$ and the rate of variation of national product $dY(t)/dt$:

$$B(t) = \varphi(dY(t)/dt), \tag{2.8}$$

where $\varphi(\cdot)$ is a non-linear function. Furthermore this accelerator is restricted by upper and lower limits, respectively denoted by U and L.

In fine, the Goodwin model also yields a mixed difference-differential equation; its solution consists of a stable limit-cycle, not of sinusoidal form, depending on the U and L values.

The future Nobel Prize-winner Maurice Allais (1953, 1955, 1956) also conceives a very original non-linear model of the cycle. It differs from Kalecki's or Goodwin's in that it is founded on essentially monetary dynamics. In fact, the whole effort of the French theorist consists of explaining stable cycles' autogeneration on the basis of interactions between preferences for cash, defined as the opposite of the speed of money's circulation, and the quantity of bank money.

The model's fundamental equation is[6]:

$$D(t + T) - D(t) = \frac{1}{T}[M(t) - M_D(t)], \tag{2.9}$$

[6]All the notations used are Allais's (1955).

where $D(t)$ represents global expenditure at the instant t, T is the time lag between revenue and spending, $M(t) - M_D(t)$ is the difference between actual money balances and desired money balances in t.

Then it is supposed that the money supply is a positive monotonically increasing function, denoted by g, of what Allais called "the psychological expansion rate", noted as $v(t)$:

$$M(t) = g(v(t)). \tag{2.10}$$

In the same way, the desired reception is by hypothesis in the form

$$M_D(t) = D(t)f(u(t)), \tag{2.11}$$

where f is a positive monotonically increasing function of $u(t)$, i.e. of the rate of economic expansion. Taking into account (2.10) and (2.11), (2.9) then becomes:

$$T[D(t+T) - D(t)] = [g(v(t)) - D(t)f(u(t))]. \tag{2.12}$$

This mixed difference-integral equation is only dependent on $D(t)$ and permits us to determine the path of the global spending (equal to revenue) in time. Its analysis shows that the model may have two types of solution: either converging towards stable or unstable equilibrium, or else towards a limit-cycle, the properties of which must be numerically computed.

In the end, as Allais indicated (1947, 1998, p. 124), "The longer past memory is, the stronger is the tendency to stability and the longer the limit-cycle period."

2.4 The Statistical and Econometric Approaches

If we can date back to Juglar and Jevons the use of long series to characterise the economic cycle, the credit for the first really statistical analysis of these series has to go to Moore and Persons.

2.4.1 The First Steps

Moore (1914) used the periodogram to detect two cycles of a respective duration of eight and 33 years in the rainfalls in the Ohio Valley. As for Persons (1919), he seems to be the first economist to have proposed to split time series into four components: the trend, the cycle, seasonality and a purely accidental hazard. We will return to the other great contribution of Persons to the analysis of fluctuations: the construction of the "Harvard barometer".

However, as early as 1913, Wesley Clair Mitchell published the first book totally devoted to the study of economic oscillations (business cycles). He developed a new methodological approach which he summed up as follows: "To observe, analyze, and systematize the phenomena of prosperity, crisis, and depression is the chief task" (Mitchell 1913, p. 20). From this position, there was no need to decide between the different cycle theories; they need only be used to select the relevant facts.

In 1920, Mitchell became the Director of the National Bureau of Economic Research, an institution which in 1921 launched a statistical research programme on economic cycles. This programme resulted in another book by Mitchell called *Business Cycles: The Problem and its Setting* (1927). In it, Mitchell criticised the use of statistical techniques—periodogram or decomposition of time series—applied by Moore and Persons; he considered that these techniques did not directly measure the business cycle. Moreover *Business Cycles* presented a synthesis of research works on the cycle undertaken in the 1920s and ended with a proposed plan for measuring economic fluctuations. Hence, as Morgan (1990, p. 50) wrote, the book "fully established Mitchell's reputation as the preeminent figure in statistical business cycle research of the interwar period".

Another book resulted from Mitchell's research programme, *Measuring Business Cycles*, written in collaboration with A.F. Burns, published in 1946. In addition to a definition of the cycle, which we will come back to later, the two authors proposed—among others—a series of measures of fluctuations, or more precisely of what he called the reference cycle on the one hand and the specific cycles on the other. The latter were connected with specific variables and were obtained by dating turnaround points of the variable under study. The reference cycle is the global, aggregated economic cycle defined on the basis of a set of relevant variables.

However, in the 1920s, Mitchell was not the only economist preoccupied by the statistical analysis of swings. The aforementioned Persons was entrusted by the Harvard Committee for Economic research in 1917 with initiating a study of the "methods for collecting and interpreting economic statistics". Two years later he published the results of his work as a monthly business barometer in the *Review of Economic Statistics*, created in 1919 by the Harvard Committee and which became in 1949 the *Review of Economics and Statistics*. This barometer relied on three cycle indicators representing the movement of the economy and covering respectively the stock market, industry and the monetary conditions. These indicators led to the famous curves called Harvard A-B-C which were supposed to represent the dynamics of economic fluctuations and therefore to forecast crises. Harvard barometers did not survive the Great Depression; however, see Samuelson (1987) for a reappraisal of the Harvard work.

During the 1920s there was a real blossoming of institutions dedicated to research on the cycle and the economic situation. In 1920 the Moscow Institute, chaired by Kondratieff, was created; one in Stockholm in 1922, in Paris and London in 1923, Berlin in 1925, etc. In January 1927 the Austrian Research Institute on Business Cycles (Österreichische Konjunkturinstitut) was created at Ludwig von Mises' behest. Thanks to his support, Hayek was its director until he left Vienna for London in 1931, when he was hired by the London School of Economics. Morgenstern succeeded him until 1938, when he immigrated to the United States after *Anschluss*.

Mitchell and Persons' intellectual influence on most of these new institutions is quite obvious, yet their futures turned out to be diverse: the Moscow institute was closed in 1928 and Kondratieff was banished to Siberia; the European institutes as well as Harvard's lost their credibility, as they had been unable to predict the 1929–1930 crisis.

2.4.2 The "Tinbergen Moment"

The decline of economic research institutes paved the way for attempts at modelling cycles. The most obvious name which comes to mind in that respect is that of Jan Tinbergen, the first Nobel Prize winner in economics in 1969, together with Ragnar Frisch. The Dutch economist's research, considerable as it is, did not come out of the blue, it was directly prepared by the work of three authors, namely Yule, Slutsky and Frisch.

Yule (1926) had showed that one had to be very careful when calculating correlations (in a statistical sense) between chronological series: these might prove to be nonsense correlations. Of course such a criticism implicitly questioned the works of the cycle analysts which were based on the calculation of high correlation coefficients to provide evidence of the relations between variables. The following year, Yule published another article in which he compared the cycle to a "pendulum bombarded with green peas", the swings being due to random shocks, represented by the green peas.

The Russian economist Slutsky (1937), in an article written in 1927 but which was published in English only in 1937, stressed even more strongly the importance of random shocks, as, by accumulating, they might produce series which could be compared to a combination of sinusoidal swings. Kuznets (1929, p. 274), who might have read Slutsky's article in its original version, came to the conclusion that "if cycles arise from random events, (…), then we obviously do not need the hypothesis of an independent regularly recurrent cause".

Ragnar Frisch, the first Nobel Prize winner in economics together with Tinbergen, is the third author who had a significant influence on the Dutch economist. In 1933 in the paper written for the book to pay homage to Cassel, he proposed a small dynamic macro-economic model of the cycle: from a mathematics perspective it was a mixed system of recurrence equations and differential equations. The attempt was completely in the *Zeitgeist*, as the 1929 crisis had focused economists' attention somewhat.

Without going into details, we can say that Frisch's model combines deterministic dynamic relations and random shocks. We could almost call it an econometric model, except that its structural parameters were not evaluated but "calibrated". Nevertheless with this type of calibration, Frisch's system proposed solutions for the three main variables and these solutions were composed of a trend and three cycles, one of which—primary—had a 8.57 year duration. This matched reality quite well.

Following up on these three authors, Jan Tinbergen designed and assessed the first econometric model of the cycle. He did it at the request of the *Vereniging voor de Staathuishoudkunde en de Statistiek*, the association of Dutch economists which convened in October 1936 a congress on the topic "Out of Depression". Tinbergen (1936), addressing an audience not very knowledgeable in quantitative methods, left out the most technical aspects of his presentation. However, one year later he published with Hermann in Paris a complete presentation of the "Dutch econometric model" and identified the quantitative effects of a large scope of measures of economic policy. Plainly, it was for the time both a major intellectual and numerical performance: the model used 31 variables and 22 equations; among the latter 16 were behavioural or technical relations which Tinbergen evaluated for the period 1923–1935 (Tinbergen 1937, pp. 14–15).

The Dutch economist took an early interest in the issue of economic fluctuations, as evidenced in particular by his contribution to *Econometrica* (Tinbergen 1935). It is therefore not surprising that the future Nobel laureate was asked in 1936 by the League of Nations to test empirically the business cycle theories as they were to be presented in Haberler (1937). Tinbergen worked two full years on this issue and published the result of his work in 1939 as two volumes entitled *Statistical Testing of Business-Cycle Theories*. The first one contained a methodological part in Chaps. 2 and 6 as well as three case studies (investment swings, residual construction and net investment in the railways); the second volume proposed an econometric model of the American economy aimed at assessing the various analyses of the business cycles.

This dynamic macro-economic model, even more than the Dutch model of 1936, was a real achievement: it contained 71 variables, 48 equations and covered the period 1919–1932; moreover it was of a higher empirical interest as Tinbergen was able to express in equations a series of theories expressed in purely verbal terms and to test them later following a three-step procedure. Of course the assessment of these various models depended on the data used (it was not very good) as well as on the specific character of the period under study (the "great depression"). But Tinbergen could not be held responsible for those.

What is more interesting from a present-day point of view is the first volume considered from its methodological dimension. The method used was called by Tinbergen "correlation analysis" (1939, vol. I, p. 15). In fact the aim was simply to assess the coefficients of a multiple linear regression (possibly with lagged variables) by minimising residual sum of squares. This estimated equation is then characterized by the correlation coefficient—the famous R^2 of modern econometricians—whose value varies from 0 to 1. The closer to unity the correlation coefficient, the better the statistical fit.

The last step in this approach consists of testing the statistical significance of coefficients. From that viewpoint, Tinbergen (1939, vol. I, p. 28) did not refer to the Neyman-Pearson theory but to what he called the "classical method", the "final formula (of which) was provided by R.A. Fischer". In practice, the method amounts to applying a t-test to each coefficient divided by its standard error. Tinbergen used also another testing method created by Frisch (1934) the method of the *bunch maps,* which has since not been used for a very long time and which we will therefore not comment on here. (The interested reader can check Tinbergen 1939 vol. I, pp. 29–31, or Valavanis 1959, pp. 146–150 for further information.)

Tinbergen's work raised different types of comments. Allen (1940), for instance, was a strong supporter but Milton Friedman (1940) was much more critical, although his review of *Statistical Testing* concerned only volume II. The severest review is without doubt Keynes' (1939). In addition to divergences on the epistemological value of Tinbergen's work, the author of the *General Theory* raised six points of criticism of the econometric methodology used: the need to determine all "causes", i.e. all explanatory variables present in a multiple regression; the inability to take into account non measurable qualitative variables; the possibility of connecting explanatory variables, which we would call today multicolinearity; the non-checking of the linearity assumption; the difficulty to correctly determine the number of lags in the assessed equations; the dependence on these estimates on the time coverage.

Tinbergen (1940) replied to the Cambridge economist; however the true reply came later with the development of the econometric theory and practice, which made it possible to solve the—real—problems raised by Keynes. For instance, it is nowadays usual to estimate non-linear equations or models with qualitative variables.

2.4.3 Towards Large Scale Models

This Keynesianism was bound to permeate in the end the whole macro-economic field. We have already mentioned above that the author of the *General Theory* was very critical of the pioneering work of Tinbergen. In the 1940s however, Haavelmo (1944) gave a new direction to econometrics by encouraging a "probabilistic revolution". The word "revolution" was used, among others, by Morgan (1990), because his approach provided a frame, a theoretical (probabilistic and statistical) structure which made it possible to test competing economic theories. It is worth noticing that Haavelmo (1943) defended Tinbergen against Keynes. In fact Haavalmo's programme was to take shape in the work of the Cowles Commission, in particular in Koopmans' (1950) and Hood and Koopmans' (1953) monographs.

Hence, when Lawrence R. Klein prolonged Tinbergen's work (1939) for the United States, he did it under different conditions characterised by the hegemony of Keynesian macro-economics and the "probabilistic revolution". His *Economic Fluctuations in the United States*[7]—Klein (1950)—developed the first Keynesian macro-economic model. It was followed by many others, in particular Klein-Goldberger's (1955) and large-scale ones, such as Brookings'.

[7]Here is Klein's (1966, pp. 227) description of the origin of his *Fluctuations*...: "(...) I was stimulated by J. Marschak to build a Tinbergen type model for the United States economy, just after completing the original version of the *Keynesian Revolution.*"

However, this type of model did not succeed in endogenously creating an oscillatory behaviour of the economy. As Adelman and Adelman (1959) showed using the example of Klein-Goldberger's system of equations, it is only by introducing random shocks that one could generate cycles, the characteristics of which could be compared to those of the American economy.

References

Adelman, I., & Adelman, F. L. (1959). The dynamic properties of the Klein-Goldberger model. *Econometrica, 27*, 596–625.

Aftalion, A. (1913). *Les crises générales et périodiques de surproduction, 2 vols*. Paris: M. Rivière et Cie.

Allais, M. (1947, 1998). *Economie et Intérêt*, second edition, Clément Juglar, Paris, 1998.

Allais, M. (1953). Illustration de la Théorie des Cycles Economiques par des Modèles Monétaires non linéaires. *Econometrica, 20*, 116–120.

Allais, M. (1955). Explication des Cycles Economiques par un Modèle Linéaire à Régulation Retardée. *Metroeconomica, 8*, 4–83.

Allais, M. (1956). Explication des cycles économiques par un modèle non linéaire à Régulation retardée. In *Les Modèles Dynamiques en Econométrie* (pp. 259–308, Vol. 62). Paris: CNRS, 1956.

Allen, R. G. D. (1940). Review of Jan Tinbergen, *Statistical Testing of Business Cycle Theories*, Vols I and II. *Economica, 7*, 335–339.

Bairoch, P. (1997). *Victoires et déboires. Histoire économique et sociale du monde du XVI siècle à nos jours*, Gallimard, Paris, tome 2.

Burns, A. F., & Mitchell, W. C. (1946). *Measuring business cycles*. New York: National Bureau of Economic Research.

Friedman, M. (1940). Review of Jan Tinbergen, Statistical Testing of Business Cycle Theories, Vol. II: Business Cycles in the United States of America, 1919-1932. *American Economic Review, 30*, 450–454.

Frisch, R. (1934). *Statistical confluence analysis by means of complete regression systems*, Universitetets Ökonomiske Institutt, Publ. n° 5, Oslo.

Frisch, R., & Holme, H. (1935). The characteristic solutions of mixed difference and differential equation. *Econometrica, 3*, 225–239.

Goodwin, R. M. (1951). The non-linear accelerator and the persistence of business cycles. *Econometrica, 19*, 1–17.

Haavelmo, T. (1943). Statistical testing of business-cycle theories. *Review of Economic Statistics, 25*, 13–18.

Haavelmo, T. (1944). « The Probability Approach in Econometrics », supplement à *Econometrica*, 12.

Haberler, G. (1937). *Prosperity and depression*. Geneva: League of Nations.

Hansen, A. H. (1941). *Fiscal policy and business cycles*. New York: W.W. Norton & Company.

Harrod, R. F. (1936). *The trade cycle. An essay*, Reprints of Economic Classics, Augustus M. Kelley, New York, 1965.

Hayek, F. A. (1928). Equilibre intertemporel de prix et mouvements de valeur de la monnaie. *Revue française d'économie, 6*(1992), 105–149.

Hayek, F. A. (1931). *Prices and production*. London, UK: George Routledge and Sons Ltd.

Hicks, J. (1950). *A contribution to the theory of the trade cycle*. Oxford: At the Clarendon Press.

Hicks, J. R. (1967). « The Hayek Story », *Critical Essays in Monetary Theory*, Oxford University Press, Oxford, 1972, pp. 203–215.

Hicks, J. (1981). Are there economic cycles?. In J Hicks (Ed.). (1982). *Collected essays on economic theory* (Vol. II), *Money, interest and wages*. Harvard University Press, 1982.

Hicks, J. (1989). *A market theory of money*. Oxford: At the Clarendon Press.
Hood, W. C., & Koopmans, T. C. (Eds.). (1953). *Studies in econometric methods, cowles commission monograph 14*. New York: Wiley.
Jevons, W. S. (1884). *Investigations in currency and finance*. London: Macmillan and co.
Juglar, C. (1862). *Des crises commerciales et de leur retour périodique en France, en Angleterre et aux Etats-Unis*. Paris: Guillaumin et Cie.
Kaldor, N. (1940). A model of the trade cycle. *Economic Journal, 50*(1940), 78–92.
Kalecki, M. (1935a). A macrodynamic theory of business cycles. *Econometrica, 3*, 327–344.
Kalecki, M. (1935b). Essai d'une théorie du mouvement cyclique des affaires, *Revue d'économie politique*, 49ème année, pp. 285–305.
Kalecki, M. (1936). Pare Uwag o Teorri Keynesa. *Ek, 3*, 18–26.
Kalecki, M. (1943a). *Studies in economic dynamics*, Allen & Unwin, London, reproduit in *Collected Works of Michal Kalecki*, vol. II, Clarendom Press, Oxford, 1991.
Kalecki, M. (1943b). Political aspects of full employment, *Political Quarterly, 14*(4), 322–331, reproduit in *Collected works of Michal Kalecki*, vol. I, Clarendom Press, Oxford, 1990, pp. 347–356.
Kalecki, M. (1954), *Theory of Economic Dynamics: An Essay on Cyclical and Long-run Changes in Capitalist Economy*, Allen & Unwin, London, reproduit in *Collected Works of Michal Kalecki* (Vol. II). Oxford: Clarendom Press, 1991.
Keynes, J. (1936). *The general theory of employment, interest, and money*. New York: Harvest/Harcourt, 1991.
Keynes, J. M. (1939). Professor tinbergen's method. *Economic Journal, 49*, 558–568.
Klein, L. R. (1949, 1966). *The keynesian revolution* (second edition). London: The Macmillan Press Ltd, 1966.
Klein, L. R. (1950). *Economic fluctuations in the United States 1921–1941I, Cowles Commission Monograph 11*. New York: Wiley.
Klein, L. R., & Goldberger, A. S. (1955). *An econometric model of the United States 1929–1952*. Amsterdam: North-Holland Publishing Company.
Koopmans, T. C. (1950). *Statistical inference in dynamic economic models, cowles commission monograph 10*. New York: Wiley.
Kuznets, S. (1929). Random events and cyclical oscillations. *Journal of the American Statistical Association, 24*, 258–275.
Malthus, T. R. (1820). *Principes d'économie politique considérés sous le rapport de leur application pratique*. Paris: Calmann-Lévy, 1969.
Marx, K. (1894), *Capital. A critique of political economy* (Vol. III). *The process of capitalist production as a whole*. New York: International Publishers, (n.d.).
Mill, J. (1848, 1871). *Principles of political economy with some of their applications to social philosophy*. Augustus M. Kelley, Fairfield, 1987.
Mises, Lv. (1912). *The theory of money and credit*. New Haven: Yale University Press.
Mises, Lv. (1966). *Human action, a treatise on economics* (third revised edition ed.). New Haven, USA: Yale University Press.
Mises, Lv. (1990). *Money, method and the market process*. Dordrecht: Kluwer Academic Publishers.
Mitchell, W. C. (1913). *Business cycles and their causes*. Berkeley: California University Memoirs.
Moore, H. L. (1914). *Economic cycles. Their Law and Cause*. New York: Macmillan.
Morgan, M. S. (1990). *The history of econometric ideas*. Cambridge: Cambridge University Press.
Nordhaus, W. D. (1975). The political business cycle. *Review of Economic Studies, 42*, 169–190.
Persons, W. M. (1919). Indices of business conditions. *Review of Economic Statistics, 1*, 5–110.
Ricardo, D. (1817, 1819, 1821). On the principles of political economy and taxation. In P. Sraffa (Ed.), *The works and correspondence of David Ricardo* (Vol. 1). Cambridge: Cambridge University Press, 1951. (Trad. franç.: *Des principes de l'économie politique et de l'impôt*, Flammarion, Paris, 1992.).

Samuelson, P. A. (1939). Interactions between the multiplier analysis and the principle of acceleration. *Review of Economic Statistics, 21*, 75–78.

Samuelson, P. A. (1987). Paradise lost and refound: The harvard ABC Barometers. *Journal of Portfolio Management, 4*, 4–9.

Say, J. -B. (1815–1821). *Cours d'économie politique et autres essais*. Paris: Flammarion, 1996.

Schumpeter, J. (1939). *Business cycles. A theoretical, historical and statistical analysis of the capitalist process*. London: McGraw-Hill Book Co.

Schumpeter, J. (1954). *History of economic analysis*. Oxford: Oxford University Press.

Selten, R., & Güth, W. (1982). Game theoretical analysis of wage bargaining in a simple business cycle model. *Journal of Mathematical Economics, 10*, 177–195.

Sismondi, L. (1827). *Nouveaux principes d'économie politique* (2ème édition). Paris: Delaunay.

Slutsky, E. (1937). The summation of random causes as the source of cyclic processes. *Econometrica, 5*, 105–146.

Tinbergen, J. (1935). Annual survey: Suggestions on quantitative business cycle theory. *Econometrica, 3*, 241–308.

Tinbergen, J. (1936). Kan hier te lande, al dan niet na Overheidsingrijpen, een verbetering van de binnenlandse conjunctuur intreden, ook zonder verbetering van onze exportpositie », *Prae-adviezen voor de Vereniging voor de Staathuishoudkunde en de Statistiek*, 's Gravenhage, pp. 62–108; traduit en anglais sous le titre « An Economic Policy for 1936. In L. H. Klaassen, L. M. Koyck & H. J. Witteveen (Eds.), *Jan Tinbergen: Selected Papers*, North-Holland, Amsterdam, 1959.

Tinbergen, J. (1937). *An econometric approach to business cycle problems*. Paris: Hermann.

Tinbergen, J. (1939). *Statistical testing of business-cycle theories*, Vol. I: *A Method and its Application to Investment Activity*; (Vol. II: *Business Cycles in the United States of America, 1919–1932*, League of Nations, Genève.

Tinbergen, J. (1940). On a method of statistical business cycle research: A reply. *Economic Journal, 50*, 141–154.

Valavanis, S. (1959). *Econometrics. An introduction to maximum likelihood*. New York: Mc Graw-Hill.

Yule, G. U. (1926). Why do sometimes get nonsense correlations between time series? A study in sampling and the nature of time series. *Journal of the Royal Statistical Society, 89*, 1–64.

Chapter 3
Empirics

Abstract From a theoretical point of view, the period after World War II was dominated by what was called the "neo-classical synthesis". Questioning the neo-classical synthesis led also to a multiplication of non-orthodox trends. In the 1970s, the Box-Jenkins root gave birth to time series econometrics which brought about a new way of looking at business cycles. In extension an important debate, launched in the early 1980s and still alive, was to feed the world of economists and statisticians.

Keywords Business cycles · Empirics · History of economic thought · Neo-classical synthesis · Time series analysis · Unorthodox theories

The first half of the 1970s appears retrospectively as the golden age of macro-econometric modelling. However, already at the beginning of that decade the analysis of time series made considerable progress. Box and Jenkins (1970) in particular, relied on the previous works of Yule and Wold and developed a forecasting methodology based on the use of stochastic processes of the ARMA type. Formally, if y_t is the observed value in t of the y series, then an ARMA (p,q) model will be represented by

$$y_t - \phi_1 y_{t-1} - \cdots - \phi_p y_{t-p} = \varepsilon_t - \theta_1 \varepsilon_{t-1} - \cdots - \theta_q y_{t-q}, \qquad (3.1)$$

where ε_t is a series of random disturbances, distributed identically and independently. The left-hand member of (3.1) is the autoregressive part of the model and the right-hand member is its moving average part. It is immediately obvious what separates such essentially atheoritical models from simultaneous equation systems, characteristic of the Cowles Commission approach.

Nelson (1972), using Box-Jenkins' methodology, showed for the period 1956–1966 that the forecast developed with univariate models of the AR(I)MA class

T. Aimar et al., *Business Cycles in the Run of History*,
SpringerBriefs in Economics, DOI 10.1007/978-3-319-24325-2_3

most of the time outclassed those resulting from the "big" FMP model (FMP is the abbreviated name of the macro-econometric model devised by the Federal Reserve, MIT and the University of Pennsylvania).

The Box-Jenkins root gave birth to Time Series econometrics which brought about a new way of looking at business cycles. The conference sponsored by the Federal Reserve Bank which took place in Minneapolis in 1975 and the proceedings of which were published two years later was quite representative of this tendency. Sims (1977, p. 1), who edited the proceedings, declared straight away that[1] "the methods now used for most quantitative macroeconomic policy analysis are fundamentally deficient." In addition to this, the author specified that there were two main ways both out of the pitfalls of macro-econometric deficiencies and to identify the cycle models correctly: 1. To use more elaborate statistical methods to take into account the dynamic dimension of these models, a dimension which was largely ignored by the "static" economic theory; 2. To pay much more attention to the logic of optimal behaviour under uncertainty and hence not to exclude "any variable in the system from the equation on the basis of a priori theory, because all variables in the system will in general affect expectations."

Sims sided of course with the second approach, which induced him to suggest the use of "vector auto-regressions" (VAR) which was nothing but a multidimensional generalisation of autoregressive models (cf. Sims 1980a). In fact their shape came down to a system of dynamic equations:

$$\mathbf{y}_t = \mathbf{A}_1\mathbf{y}_{t-1} + \cdots + \mathbf{A}_p\mathbf{y}_{t-p} + \mathbf{u}_t, \tag{3.2}$$

where $\mathbf{y}_t = (\mathbf{y}_{1t}, \ldots, \mathbf{y}_{Kt})$, the $\mathbf{A}_i$,$i = 1, \ldots, p$, are $K \times K$ matrices of coefficients and $\mathbf{u}_t = (u_{1t}, \ldots, u_{Kt})$, is a white noise vector or innovations of average $\mathbf{0}$ and of variance-covariance matrix $\boldsymbol{\Omega}_u$. By Wold's theorem, any VAR model—stationary, we will come back to this later—allows an infinite moving average representation:

$$\mathbf{y}_t = \sum_{j=0}^{+\infty} \Theta_j \mathbf{u}_{t-j}. \tag{3.3}$$

In this case, if we interpret innovations as shocks to endogenous variables, they are propagated dynamically throughout the system. The effect of shock $\mathbf{u}_t$ on the vector $\mathbf{y}_{t-s}, s > 0$ is then given by the matrix of general element:

$$\theta_{ij,t+s} = \frac{\partial y_{i,t+s}}{\partial u_{jt}}. \tag{3.4}$$

We can directly interpret (3.4) as follows: the multiplier θ_{ij} measures the response of the i-th endogenous variable to an impulse, a shock in j happening s periods previously. From these multipliers we obtain what are called impulse response functions.

[1] Sims hid cautiously behind the opinion of "economists who were experiencing new statistical methods".

Thus is the type of model Sims (1980b) used to compare the American (and also the German) cycle between and after the wars.

One can see, however, where the rub is in modelling: a VAR is by principle atheoretical. Hence, as Cooley and Le Roy (1985) noted, the tool was incapable of testing theories (of the cycle, for instance) but also of analysing the impact of economic policy measures. Another criticism, of a statistical type, cannot be discarded: the construction of response functions and the estimation of parameters of the model by least squares rely on the assumption of time series stationarity.[2]

From this point of view, an important debate launched in the early 1980s was to feed the world of economists and statisticians. It had been known for a long time that many series incorporated a linear trend and as we saw, Persons (1919) was probably the first economist to propose splitting them into different components, one of them being the cycle. As a direct result, many practitioners extracted the trend through empirical smoothing or regression methods (it is sometimes fallacious to use Granger and Newbold's wording, 1974), and the cycle was then measured as the gap to the deterministic trend. Nelson and Plosser's seminal article (1982) was to question such an approach of non-stationarity and to introduce a second class of non stationary, purely stochastic processes, which followed a random path denoted as $y_t = y_{t-1} + \varepsilon_t$, where ε_t is a white noise, i.e. a stationary process. It was then possible to oppose the two classes of processes as follows:

$$\begin{cases} y_t = \alpha + \beta t + \varepsilon_t \\ y_t = y_{t-1} + \varepsilon_t. \end{cases} \tag{3.5}$$

Obviously in order to stationarise the first process in (3.5), one should simply deduct the straight line $\alpha + \beta t$ from y_t. This is the reason why Nelson and Plosser (1982, p. 141) called such processes *trend-stationary* (TS). On the other hand, differencing the random walk yields $\Delta y_t = y_t - y_{t-1} = \varepsilon_t$. As ε_t is stationary, so is Δy_t Consequently, such a process can be made stationary by simple; it is then called DS (*difference stationary*). The distinction is important: if the process is TS, the cycle is represented by a set of transitory and regular fluctuations of the growth path around the deterministic tendency; on the other hand if a process is DS, the underlying tendency is stochastic, which implies that shocks have a permanent impact on the series, which will not come back to its original trajectory.

The problem then comes down to testing the null hypothesis of a DS process as opposed to the alternative hypothesis of a TS process. Unit root tests developed first by Fuller (1976), Dickey and Fuller (1979, 1981) are used to that end. Nelson and Plosser reached the conclusion that of the 14 macro-economic series they studied, all but one, the unemployment rate, have unit roots and consequently are affected lastingly by shocks of a permanent character.

On the basis of this analysis, many research works—Beveridge and Nelson (1981), Campbell and Mankiw (1987), Perron (1988), Harvey (1989),

[2]Intuitively a series is stationary (of the second order) if the mean and the variance are constant and if the autocovariances do not depend on time.

etc.—developed new extraction methods of the business cycle. A note of caution is needed here: several of these studies, including Perron (1989), Zivot and Andrews (1992), Lumsdaine and Papell (1997), based on the existence of structural breaks in Nelson and Plosser's (1982) series, had to relativize and qualify the results obtained by the latter: for instance Plosser (1989) counted only three series with unit roots, Lumsdaine and Papell (1997) eight, etc. The debate on that issue is far from being closed.

3.1 Towards New Approaches of the Cycle

3.1.1 The Decomposition of the Neo-Classical Synthesis

From a theoretical point of view, the Thirty Glorious Years were dominated by what was called the "neo-classical synthesis", i.e. a combination of Keynesian macroeconomics and of marginalistic micro-economic analysis. Joan Robinson was probably right to name this trend "neo-neoclassical", since the marginalists are themselves neo-classics compared to the Ricardian school and its successors. However, such complicated wording is just impossible to use.

Two economists were responsible for this synthesis: on the one hand Hicks with *Mister Keynes and the Classics* (1937) and *Value and Capital* (1939); and on the other Samuelson (1948) with his *Foundations of Economic Analysis*. To these two names should be added Patinkin (1956), although he played a smaller role. Two other notables, Samuelson and Solow (1960) completed the macro-economic Keynesian model with a Phillips curve. To these, we can add Friedman and his 1964 "plucking model" (see the revised 1993 version). It is an original treatment of the natural output rate. In Friedman's model, output holds steady at a maximum value, i.e. the full employment value, and is occasionally plucked downward through a negative demand shock. It is an asymmetric alternative to the self-generating symmetric cyclical process often used to explain contractions and subsequent revivals. Friedman likens the path of output to a string attached to the underside of an upward sloping board, to represent the path's feasible ceiling, which is plucked downward at irregular intervals. However, the neo-classical synthesis was strongly questioned at the turn of the 1970s. The reasons are a mixture of increased inflation, the return of recessions and financial accidents, stagflation, a hybrid of a simultaneous increase of the unemployment rate and the inflation rate, the breaking up of the Bretton Woods system, etc. All these factors gave rise to a groundswell against Keynesian macro-economics and to a blossoming of new explanations of the cycle.

Thus the monetarist school opposed Keynesian interventionism; money started to play a predominant role in the analysis of economic fluctuations. Following his theory of permanent revenue, Friedman put forward an explanatory principle of the cycle, which applied to any asset; the specificity of money is its exogenous offer. In case there was an increase in the quantity of money, the agents who tried and maximised their utility adjusted their portfolios between the various assets, thus following the principles of the permanent income theory.

As money creation would have induced an unbalance in agents' assets, money had real effects on the economy because of the agents' will to get back to an optimal patrimonial structure. The analysis of the cycle relied entirely on the disconnection of permanent income and observed income. Hence this monetarist trend questioned the long term arbitration between inflation and unemployment, except if one was to continuously increase the inflation growth rate. Only in the short run are agents sensitive to money illusion. In the long run, monetary stimulus (expansion) entails only a shift of the Phillips curve. The curve is vertical and defines the natural unemployment rate. It is impossible to arbitrate between unemployment and inflation with such a curve.

3.1.2 Equilibrium Cycles

Friedman's development of this idea was further investigated by the school of rational expectations (*equilibrium business cycles*). Lucas, Sargent and Wallace provided the theoretical foundations of the criticism against the Phillips curve. It was obviously Lucas (1976) who expressed the most severe attack against all current macro-economic models. Lucas criticised the lack of micro-economic foundations in the Keynesian based models. Economic variables resulted from individual choices conditioned by expectations on the future state of the economy. It was essential to take into account the way people constructed these expectations, otherwise it would be impossible to devise any economic policy.

As early as 1973, Lucas devised a model based on imperfect information and rational expectations. The Walrasian paradigm was abandoned; agents were supposed to have an imperfect vision of prices, after all. The starting point of the analysis rested on a big scale economy and decentralised markets. Hence agents took part in micro-markets and had only very imperfect information on the other markets and the price system. Their perception of random shocks could lead them to false interpretations of the price signals and to undertaking actions which would disturb the whole economic system.

Lucas' supply curve defined the product as a decreasing function of the price surprise, i.e. the unexpected rise of the general price level; it was Lucas' criticism of the Phillips curve. As a consequence, non-anticipated inflation could lead an individual to believe that the relative price of his output had increased and therefore be tempted to increase production. The result was a money-based cycle around a long term growth path which characterised an economy at equilibrium. The money supply caused shocks to the system, leading to cyclical fluctuations, here, equilibrium cycles, where the propagation of the cycle can only originate in the agents' optimizing behaviour, in reaction to shock. It was not enough to introduce shocks in the Keynesian system to describe fluctuations: economic movements had to be deducted from the agents' responses to these external impulses. In fact, Lucas' analysis showed how an equilibrium model with decentralised markets and imperfect information could account for the effects of nominal shocks and real shocks on output. As for demand shocks, they had an impact on output only if they were not anticipated.

Although it was favourably received, Lucas' theory proved incapable of explaining the persistence of output gaps (see for instance Modigliani's criticism). Lucas later introduced the costs of capital formation to account for this phenomenon of persistence. But Lucas' position was not sufficiently convincing for the supporters of the theory of cycles at equilibrium, who called on other types of shocks to reproduce persistence in the observed fluctuations, namely technological shocks.

The supporters of this new line of thought, called *Real Business Cycle* (RBC), defined it as the result of an optimal adaptation of the economy to equilibrium. They revived the neo-classical explanation of economic fluctuations. Following Lucas' initial path, they aimed at integrating the concept of cycle into the Walrasian paradigm to express economic phenomena in terms of equilibrium. However they reversed Friedman's and Lucas' monetarist analyses, as they tried and showed that most fluctuations could be explained without introducing a monetary disturbance. These fluctuations were supposed to result from optimal reactions of economic agents to shocks of the total factor productivity (the overall productivity of factors). As these shocks were exogenous and random, the evolution of the cycle had to be of stochastic nature (quasi-cyclical). The economic cycle was in that case an oscillatory motion of the natural output and not the gap to the trend, since the factors which caused it were also at the source of growth. Hence the usual dichotomy between the sources of growth and the sources of fluctuations was not justified as the latter corresponded to the very variations of the natural growth rate, to the variations of productivity.

The first Real Business Cycle (RBC) models were developed by Kydland and Prescott (1982) and Long and Plosser (1983), in a complete break with the traditional view of the cycle.

Firstly, this approach considers that monetary policies have no bearing in the cycle dynamic; it also insists on the exogenous character of technological shocks.

Secondly, it considers that cycles are not an expression of disequilibrium; on the contrary, they are the gauges that measure an economy's best adjustment to equilibrium.

Lastly, it prevents cycles from being seen as variations of a same trend rather than changes to the trend. In fact, it is an integrated vision of the growth of cycles.

The RBC founding authors' project is in fact clear to the keen observer; it is to understand the cyclic evolution of the economy. To do this, the model associates a constant scale-of-economies production function with an equation of capital accumulation, added to various constraints. Concretely, the RBC theorists construct a model of calculable equilibrium. They introduce chance shocks so that the product resulting from the model's equilibrium fluctuates, as does GDP in real terms.

Concordance between the simulated fluctuations and those of the real economic variables is tested. Where it is found, the model is considered to represent the economic dynamic with a strong argument: that the cycles are thoroughly exogenous, with productivity variations coming from climate or international events.

However contestable the RBC approach, it is today a major macroeconomic research project. Its advantage obviously lies in its methodology: quantitative simulations to simplify economic representation; however, the underlying economic message in this approach, all things being equal, remains relatively weak.

3.1.3 Unorthodox Theories: Minsky

Questioning the neo-classical synthesis led also to a multiplication of non-orthodox trends. From the point of view of the cycle theories, two deserve special attention: the post-Keynesians with Hyman P. Minsky and the neo-Austrians, who continued the analyses of Hayek and von Mises.

Minsky is known today for his "financial instability hypothesis" of capitalism; in the press this was also referred to as "Minsky moment". His first book *John Maynard Keynes*, Minsky (1975), questioned the neo-classical interpretation of the *General Theory,* which Joan Robinson called "bastard Keynesianism". From then on the author was considered as one of the major figures of the post-Keynesian movement essentially defined as "return to Keynes".

Minsky took an interest in the analysis of the business cycle at an early stage. In one of his first articles on this question (Minsky 1957, p. 859), he was already critical that "the authors who have constructed these accelerator-multiplier models have paid little, if any, attention to the monetary prerequisites and effects of the assumed processes." From then on his research programme was all set: he would show how entrepreneurs and bankers motivated by the sole search for profit turned the initially robust financial system into a system subject to repeated financial crises. This programme was developed progressively, in successive steps, to reach the final synthesis to be found in Minsky (1986).

The starting point of the analysis lay with the acknowledgement of two price systems: the first one applied to current output of goods and services and the other to financial assets. These two sets of prices were linked, since on the one hand investment goods were part of the output of the period of reference and on the other hand they had a current price which had to be coherent with their prices as capital assets.

The prices of the goods produced during the on-going period were determined "à la Kalecki", by applying the mark up of the various costs, in particular the labour factor. Supply prices for the different kinds of investment goods represented a subgroup of these current prices. As for the capital assets, they were determined by supply and demand in specific markets: their supply was fixed during the current period and their demand depended on the expected cash flows during their life time. In the economy under study, there was a set of financial assets which could be considered as capital assets, since they also produced a flow of further liquid assets. For price determination see, for instance, Minsky (1986, pp. 200s).

The fact that there was a price for a capital asset or a financial asset did not automatically entail the actual corresponding investment. This investment needed also to be funded! From this point of view, Minsky distinguished between two essential sources of funding of firms: internal funds, i.e. the profit reserves of these firms on the one hand; external funds on the other hand resulting from bank loans or the emission of bonds or stocks. Loans (as bank loans or bonds) meant payment commitments; hence they corresponded to a cost, similar to paying salaries or buying intermediate goods and this cost had to be taken into account in the supply prices of the different wares. Hence—Minsky (1986, p. 207)—"the decision to invest therefore involves a supply function of investment, which depends upon labour costs and short-term interest rates, a demand function for investment, which is derived from the price of capital assets, and the anticipated structure and conditions of financing."

Firms' positions in terms of capital assets were financed by a combination of stock shares and debts. In that respect Minsky distinguished three possible regimes: hedge financing, speculative finance and Ponzi finance[3].

By reference to Minsky (1986, Appendix A, pp. 371–379), one could be tempted to formalize these three financial regimes as follows: Denote by C_i the repayments, during period i, consequent to the agreements contracted at borrowing; Q_i the anticipated quasi-rents or profit for the same period, resulting from a particular investment and by $\sigma^2_{Q_i}$ the corresponding variance. Hedge financing of a position requires that

$$C_i < Q_i - \lambda\sigma^2_{Q_i}, \quad \text{for all} \quad i, \tag{3.6}$$

where λ is such that the subjective probability associated with $Q_i < C_i$ is very small. In other words, the bigger the gap between the left-hand element of (3.6) and the right-hand one, the wider margin of security for the investor. It follows that any unit in financing by hedging will need enough cash flow from the treasury to repay the whole debt, both principal and interest.

Conversely, if the inequality

$$C_i < Q_i - \lambda\sigma^2_{Q_i}, \tag{3.7}$$

holds good for any period near i, at least in the short term, the unit in question will not have enough cash flow to be able to reimburse its debts. In that case, two behaviours are possible for the unit considered: either the liquid assets cover only the interest payment and it adopts a speculative finance mode; or it does not even have the capacity to cover the interest payment and it is compelled to call on loans, which Minsky called a "Ponzi finance" mode.[4]

[3]Charles Ponzi was a swindler of Italian origin, living in the United States, who, in 1920, offered an investment with a 50 % return within 45 days; actually he did not invest the money he was entrusted with or only a small part of it; he only paid the interests of his earlier customers with the money provided by the newcomers and so on.

[4]Minsky (1986, p. 377) specified that this type of funding "is not necessarily fraudulent".

In an economy, the heavier the weight of speculative finance and Ponzi finance, the more this economy is bound to be subject to financial crises. From a general point of view, capitalist economies experience an alternation of periods of financial robustness and fragility, according to the prevailing combination of the three types of funding. According to Minsky "serious" recessions occurred during the latter periods (Minsky 1986, p. 194).

Minsky's proposed explanation of cyclical fluctuations can be summed up as follows. During the periods of financial peace—for instance the period which followed WWII until the American "credit crunch" of 1996—characterised by an absence of speculative boom as well as by the predominance of hedge funds, the management of global demand and the intervention of central banks are sufficient to avoid very large variations in investment demand. Because of the robustness of financial structures one may be inclined to think that this state will last, which encourages the proliferation of financial innovations and of speculative behaviours. Progressively the financial structures become fragile, accidents increase, speculative and Ponzi behaviours become widespread and so does the debt. Then a period of instability starts, enhanced by the speculative boom of the stock markets. A stock market crisis follows, pulling down in its fall banks and financial institutions. The investment demand collapses and consumption declines following the fall of stock quotes and the need to reduce debts. Recession follows, which might lead to an even deeper slump… as was the case in the 1930s.

3.1.4 Unorthodox Theories: Hayek

Hayek received the Nobel Prize for his theory of economic fluctuations which had been criticised and marginalised for a long time by post-war economic thought. This reward encouraged a number of Austrian authors to pursue his analysis and bring their own contributions, e.g. Rothbard (1975) or Garrison (1986, 1989, 1997, 2001). The latter's work inspired many contemporary applications of Hayek's perspective. However these developments did not make it possible to remove some ambiguities to be found in the Austrian analysis of economic fluctuations.

The members of the Austrian school were characterised by their focus on ignorance, historical time and the subjectivism of expectations. They favoured qualitative reasoning and condemned the use of quantitativism in economics. Legend has it that Hayek was refused a position at the Chicago economics department because he was hostile to statistics, which caused Knight to veto him [Hayek gave a laconic comment on this event: "I was proposed first to the faculty of economics, but they turned me down", Hayek, in Kresge (1994, p. 128)]. The theory of economic fluctuations is in fact one of the rare incursions of the Austrians into the macro-economic area; its contemporary repercussions raise certain questions.

How can we in fact define the cycle parameters without referring to quantitative macro-economic variables? How can we identify and measure capital, express the relations of substitution and complementarity? Similarly, by which method can the shocks of monetary policy on interest, relative prices and the length of production steps be measured? Finally, how can the gap between the monetary rate and the equilibrium rate be identified and measured, since in theoretical economics this gap is only a theoretical reference which cannot be assessed? As noted by Bismans and Mougeot: "Use of econometrics, a statistical tool, requires some flexibility in pure Austrian theory" (Bismans and Mougeot 2008, p. 83).

Recent empirical applications of the Austrian cycle theory (Keeler 2001; Mulligan 2002, 2006; Cwik 1998; Hugues 1997; etc.) reflect this relaxing which sometimes is hard to reconcile with the original theory. The authors' concern is not so much to identify fluctuations using the Austrian tools, as to examine the relevance of the Hayekian explanation on the basis of stylised facts from other theories.

There is also some ambiguity at the normative level, which brings to mind the origin of the cycle. Are we dealing here with an exogenous or endogenous approach of fluctuations? Following his Nobel Prize, Hayek developed theses (1976 and 1978a) which aimed at freeing money from political manipulations. However in *Prices and Production*, he described the general architecture of credit as a pyramid-shaped structure composed of different layers, one of which was internal organisation which was difficult to regulate via direct tools. Even if the quantity of fiduciary money remained stable, it might happen that the other parts of the structure favour an increase of the issue of credit, following mechanisms which the authorities could hardly monitor. The increased supply of money in the widest sense of the term and the development of cycles are not always automatically linked to an expansionist attitude of the central banks.

There is also ambiguity about the status of equilibrium. Hayek (1928) gave some thoughts very early to the logics of intertemporal equilibriums, so that Lucas saw there an anticipation of his own work. But how can we identify empirically equilibrium from an Austrian point of view since there is no method to guarantee that all known opportunities are exploited? More fundamentally, for the Neo-Austrians (cf. Kirzner 1973, 1979, etc.), the ignorance paradigm makes it impossible to consider that all available opportunities are known and exploited. Hence there is always disequilibrium but it is not possible to know either its size or its source. From that point of view, is there really an Austrian epistemology of the cycle? How can one account for growth, or conversely for the crisis, while respecting the Austrian paradigm? The Austrians are theoreticians of disequilibrium and they provided a specific and measurable definition of the improved quality of coordination only in a negative way as the absence of intervention.

The last ambiguity concerns the explanatory or predictive status of the Austrian theory of the business cycle. Most studies elaborated after Hayek's Nobel Prize gave a retrospective view of events. Rothbard (1975) tried an Austrian reading of the 1930s crisis and the monetary phenomena which occurred before. O'Driscoll and Shenoy (1976), Garrison (2001), Cwik (1998) and Hugues (1997) used various indicators at various times and in various countries to test the explanatory capacity of the theory. Powell (2002) adopted the same approach when he applied the Austrian tools to examine the Japanese recession of 1990.

Theory and history were jointly called upon to explain specific moments. Should one then give up forecasting? However, in *The Pretence of Knowledge*, a text which corresponded to the speech he gave at the Nobel Prize ceremony, Hayek himself claimed: "I am anxious to repeat, we will still achieve predictions which can be falsified and which therefore are of empirical significance" (Hayek 1974, p. 33). But things are not as clear cut; in the same text, Hayek condemned empirical facts and specified that "because we (…) cannot know at which particular structure of prices and wages demand would everywhere equal supply, we also cannot measure the deviations from that order; nor can we statistically test our theory that it is the deviations from that 'equilibrium' system of prices and wages which make it impossible to sell some of the products and services at the prices at which they are offered" (ibid., p. 27).

3.2 Long Cycles

Since the end of the 19th century, the dream of all long cycle theorists has been to develop a general theory so good that it could serve as a code translating the meaning of present forces into terms of future movements. This remains a dream. Our knowledge of the complex body economics is still too imperfect to be codified into a handbook. The best we can do is to synthesise existing theories of why the circular flow of socio-economic moves in the rhythms that we call long movements of the Kondratieff type, Kuznets cycles, Juglar cycles etc.

3.2.1 From the Precursors

The short-term and intermediate-term economic cycle noted by Juglar (1862), Kuznets (1930) were easily perceptible fluctuations created by oversupply or excess demand for products, services, or money. C. Juglar was the first to correlate clearly perceptions of economics, statistics, and history to use them in the understanding of mechanisms of alternating prosperity and recession. C. Juglar analysed banking figures, interest rates, prices, marriage rates, and other evidence to support his notion of these major crises. He believed that he had discovered a single wave underlying the movements of world economies. More widely accepted in recent years is the 15- to 25-year swing in economic growth rates uncovered by Nobel laureate S. Kuznets. The cycle is more evident in the United States than elsewhere. Abramovitz (1961) recognises the Kuznets cycle as associated with population growth and immigration. Most economists hold that this cycle was material only for the period from 1840 to 1914.

There is another type of cycle, less perceptible because its duration is longer, its dynamics less obvious, and its origins less well defined. Economists who refer to it as the long wave or long cycle of the Kondratieff type. More than 160 years ago, H. Clarke described this longer cycle, which was different from others affecting the economies of Europe. In 1847 he published a paper in the British Railway Journal called *Physical Economy* describing fluctuations between 1793 and his own time. H. Clarke offered no explanations. He merely recorded the figures. At the beginning of the twentieth century, several economists suggested that a long economic cycle was identifiable: G. Cassel, J. van Gelderen, A. Spiethoff, S. De Wolff etc. (Diebolt 2005).

Thus, the long cycle that bears his name was not originated by N. Kondratieff. In describing the origins of his theory, N. Kondratieff wrote that he arrived at the hypothesis concerning the existence of long cycles in the years 1919–1920. Without going into a special analysis, he formulated his own thesis for the first time in his study *The World Economy and Economic Fluctuations in the War and Post-War Period*. During the winter and spring of 1925, he wrote a special study, *Long Business Cycles*, published in Moscow by the Institute of Conjuncture in 1925. N. Kondratieff worked out his theories on the basis of wholesale prices, interest on British consoles and French rents, deposits at French saving banks, French trade, *per capita* coal, wage data of English farm and textile workers and French coal miners, pig-iron production in the United States, coal consumption in France, gold production, and other production series from 1780 to 1926. He used regression analyses of quantified data and a nine-year moving average to eliminate minor fluctuations. With his development of a theory of investment cycles, N.D. Kondratieff was the first to put forward the idea that long cycles originated in the very functioning of the economic system. An increase in saving increases the possibility for investing available capital and causes the long upward period. Reduction in saving reduces investment and causes the downward swing.

3.2.2 To the Schumpeterian Tradition

Schumpeter (1939) enriched the field of interpretation of long cycles by introducing the role of innovations. Grouped in time and concentrated in a few branches of industry, innovations govern regular cycles. They first tend to attract capital, and then the diffusion of the innovations throughout the economy modifies the economic balance and increases the risk of failure for the next innovations. The economy must use a recession process to assimilate the progress of the upward phase before the system approaches equilibrium again and allows for new innovations.

From 1945 to 1970, in spite of notable work by Imbert (1959) and Weinstock (1964), less attention was paid to research on long movements of the economy because of the continuous growth observed in the economies of developed countries and the dominance of Keynesian thinking.

Since the economic downturn in the early 1970s, the theses developed by Schumpeter have experienced wide distribution (Kleinknecht 1987; Mensch 1977; Freeman 1996 etc.). From our point of view, the major works in that respect favour the role of investment tempo and innovation. The idea which underlies neo-schumpeterian logic is that the emergence of new products and processes during the long depression phase induces an investment flow connected with the renewal of equipment which in turn leads to the recovery of economic activity. When this renewal ends, the investment flow decreases again which leads to a new depression phase.

If the neo-Schumpeterian analysis provides a first approach of reality, it still ignores the major role played by the social variables in economic dynamics. However, it unfortunately pays no attention to the intermediary cycle, Kuznets's cycle which was supposed to last some 20 years and referred to the cursory but famous dating of the author (1930).

We should also mention the school of the social structure of accumulation. It appeared towards the end of the 1970s, with Gordon's pioneering work, followed by numerous other contributions (Gordon et al. 1983). This research work proposes an interpretation of the long cycles of economic activity allocating a major role to the institutional transformations which punctuated contemporary history in the developed capitalist countries. The succession of different social structures of accumulation, following a process of construction and later decline of each of the social structures of accumulation, allows us to interpret the cycles of economic and social activity.

3.3 The Empirics of Business Cycle Analysis

3.3.1 What Is the Business Cycle?

Today there is a rather general agreement on the terms of Burns and Mitchell's definition (1946, p. 3): "A cycle consists of expansions occurring at about the same time in many economic activities, followed by similarly general recessions, contractions, and revivals which merge into the expansion phase of the next cycle; this sequence of changes is recurrent but not periodic; in duration business cycles vary from more than one year to ten or twelve years".

This complex, very balanced wording contains three essential elements to define recessions and also expansion phases: (1) the decline of economic activity must be sufficiently marked; (2) it must have an impact on many sectors of the economy at stake; and (3) the contraction must last long enough, even if its duration is much shorter than the expansion phases and there is asymmetry between expansions and contractions.

However, the problem is to be able to transcribe this definition into reality, and in particular to identify the one or several series which provide for a measure of aggregate economic activity and then for identifying their turning points. For Burns and Mitchell (1946, p. 72), "aggregate activity can be given a definite meaning and made conceptually measurable by identifying it with gross national product at current prices". However the two authors specified immediately—in 1946—that this series frequency was neither monthly nor quarterly; consequently they suggested using a set of replacement series which could be used to determine the aggregate reference cycle, essentially through graphic methods, i.e. by observing clusters of turning points.

This type of approach raised two main criticisms: on the one hand the cycle was one component which had to be extracted from the reference series and not the chronicle as such; on the other hand the graphic analysis of Burns and Mitchell was exclusively empirical and did not rely on techniques of statistical inference.

The latter criticism was to be found mainly in the trend which tried to construct "coincident indicators" of the economic cycle on a probabilistic basis. The pioneering article in that area is Stock and Watson's (1991); the approach was generalised by Forni et al. (2000) with their general dynamic factor model.

The other criticism of Burns and Mitchell's approach came from all those who were trying to isolate the cyclical component in the series, using many, many methods. We are dealing here, however, with nothing more than updated versions of statistical decomposition methods of chronicles, launched, as we saw above, by Persons. They go from the determination of the "phase average trend", disseminated by the researchers of the American NBER (cf. Boschan and Ebanks 1978) to the use of multiple filters developed during the previous twenty years.

The approach common to most of these methods consists of firstly removing the trend from the series under study then isolating the cycle. Here we have left out the issue of seasonality. There are three main methods to remove the trend:

1. estimating a linear and deterministic trend and then deducting it from the series
2. differentiating the series to eliminate the stochastic trend
3. applying the Hodrick-Prescott (1997) filter.

The first two methods which, following DeJong (2007), we call respectively detrending and differencing, are based on the implicit assumption that the series under study, y_t, grows at an approximately constant rate. If we take the logarithm of the series in question, the temporal variations of In y_t are equivalent to the growth rate of y_t. Indeed $\partial \,\text{In}\, y_t/\partial t = (\partial y_t/\partial t)/y_t = \dot{y}_t/y_t = g_t$.

The "detrending" process supposes that the series has a *deterministic* trend, thus obeying a process which generates data in the form of:

$$y_t = y_0(1+g_y)^t e^{u_t}, \tag{3.8}$$

where u_t is a second-order stationary stochastic process. In logarithms, (3.8) becomes:

$$\text{In}\, y_t = \text{In}\, y_0 + t\text{In}\,(1+g_y) + u_t = \text{In}\, y_0 + g_y t + u_t, \tag{3.9}$$

as In $(1+g_y)$ can be approximated by g_y. It is easy to estimate g_y in (3.9) by ordinary least squares, then simply subtracting this trend from In y_t. The series is then said to be trend stationary.

In comparison, the differentiation method supposes that y_t has a stochastic trend and that the process generating y_t is given by

$$\begin{aligned} y_t &= y_0 e^{\varepsilon_t}, \\ \varepsilon_t &= \delta + \varepsilon_{t-1} + u_t, \end{aligned} \tag{3.10}$$

where u_t is once again a second-order stationary stochastic process. By taking the logarithms, (3.10) becomes

$$\text{In}\, y_t = \text{In}\, y_0 + \varepsilon_t. \tag{3.11}$$

The first difference of In y_t in (3.11), taking into account (3.10), is given by:

$$\text{In}\, y_t - \text{In}\, y_{t-1} = \varepsilon_t - \varepsilon_{t-1} = \delta + u_t. \tag{3.12}$$

As we have already mentioned, the In y_t series is then said to be *difference stationary*. The δ estimator is equal to the average of In y_t − In y_{t-1} which you then simply need to subtract from (3.12).

The choice between these two procedures occurs exclusively according to the decision whether the generating process is given by (3.9) or by (3.11). It is a difficult choice to make, since, as we have seen, the controversy initiated by Nelson and Plosser (1982) on the existence of a unit root is not quite conclusive.

The third approach to remove the trend of a series is Hodrick-Prescott's. It starts with the decomposition of In y_t in the form

$$\text{In}\, y_t = g_t + c_t, \tag{3.13}$$

where g_t is the growth component in In y_t and c_t its cyclic component. The following step consists to estimate the values of c_t and g_t in minimising

$$\sum_{t=1}^{T} c_t^2 + \lambda \sum_{t=1}^{T} (g_t - 2g_{t-1} + g_{t-2})^2, \tag{3.14}$$

λ being a given parameter (generally taken as equal to 1600 for quarterly series). Suppressing the trend leads in the end to:

$$\text{In}\, y_t - \hat{g}_t = \hat{c}_t \tag{3.15}$$

In addition to these three techniques, there are filters called "band-pass filters" which do not require to remove first the trend of a series in order to extract the cyclical component; the general principle of these filters—Baxter and King (1999), Christiano and Fitzgerald (2003)—is to eliminate all the cycles located outside a defined frequency spectrum (between 6 and 40 semesters). By proceeding in such a way, one would obtain an "optimal" filter; however in practice one can only get an approximation.

In the end there are as many different cycles as there are filters and even more, if one varies the specific parameters of each of these filters. This is the main criticism which can be addressed to this type of approach. One could add that it leads to fallacious fluctuations: see on that point Cogley (2006). Furthermore, when the aim is to identify the cycle, one always comes back to Burns and Mitchell's definition.

3.3.2 Measuring and Dating the Business Cycle

We close this synthesis with a major issue, i.e. the problem of dating the economic cycle. The National Bureau of Economic Research (NBER) played a major role in that respect by drawing up an official monthly chronology of the American cycle implemented by its Business Cycle Dating Committee, composed of seven specialists in economic fluctuation analysis. Their role is to identify the economic peaks and troughs that constitute the turning points in economic activity, in this case the periods of expansion and contraction. The chronology they were able to draw up on this basis—cf. NBER (2009)—goes back to 1854; the latest recession started in December 2007 and was announced by the Committee one year later on 11 December 2008. Ferrara (2009) contains a synthesis of similar attempts to date the cycle of the Euro zone.

The methodology used by the NBER relies on the analysis of eight economic series, namely, GDP, unemployment rate, industrial output, etc. However, it is not possible to see the specific weight allocated to each of these series by the Dating Committee releases, nor which decisional procedure is used, except that they are consensual. Moreover, as indicated by Romer (1994, p. 574), a former member of the Dating Committee, the methods evolved over time, in particular because the cyclical profile of the economy before 1927 was based on detrended data, which was not the case later. All in all, one is forced to the conclusion that the NBER dating process was largely subjective.

In order to make the method more objective, several competing approaches arose. They can be gathered into four big categories: univariate procedures to detect the turning points, either automated or based on a parametric model; multivariate procedures, either automated or model-based.

Computing the peaks and troughs of a time series to determine the cycle is an old game which dates back to the pioneering work of Bry and Boschan (1971). A complete description of the method used and its programming (in fortran) was given by the two authors: see in particular Bry and Boschan (1971, pp. 19–29). Here is a simplified version:

Let y_t be a monthly series. If it is a continuous function, its peaks (and its troughs) are local maximums (minimums) of this function. To transpose this criterion to y_t, in fact discrete in economics, we introduce the indicator function $\mathbf{1}_A$ which has a value of 1 with event A and a value of 0 without it. If P_t *and* C_t are binary variables equal to the unit respectively when a peak and a trough are reached and equal to zero in all other cases, then:

$$P_t = \mathbf{1}_{\{y_t < y_{i \pm j}, j=1,\ldots,k\}} \tag{3.16}$$

$$C_t = \mathbf{1}_{\{y_t < y_{i \pm j}, j=1,\ldots,k\}} \tag{3.17}$$

Bry-Boschan's (BB) algorithm goes through three stages:

1. Smoothing the series using a rolling average over a 12 month period and determining a number of turning points with (3.16) and (3.17) and $k = 5$.
2. Eliminate the return points which do not represent a complete cycle (from peak to peak or from trough to trough) of at least 15 months.
3. Make sure that the peaks and troughs alternate by removing successive repeats (e.g.: if two peaks follow each other, only use the one of higher value).

The computer programme used by Bry-Boschan gave way to much faster algorithms, such as James Engel's (written in MATLAB and in GAUSS, available at www.ncer.edu.au). Harding and Pagan (2002) devised a quarterly version (called BBQ) which can be applied to the quarterly GDP series; it is essentially the same except that there is no preliminary smoothing of the series, that k is taken equal to two quarters, and a complete cycle has to cover at least five quarters.

The algorithm which has just been described is independent of any model. However, following Hamilton (1989) one can express the hypothesis that the trajectory of y_t is governed by a Markov regime-switching model. More concretely let us assume that y_t can be modelled by an AR(1) process:

$$y_t = c_{s_t} + \phi y_{t-1} + \varepsilon_t, \quad \varepsilon_t \sim IID(0, \sigma^2), \tag{3.18}$$

where s_t is a non-observed (latent) random variable, with a value of 1 or 2 depending on whether the economy is expanding or contracting.

How do we get from $s_t = 1$ to $s_t = 2$ and vice versa? The simplest probabilistic specification is to suppose that the trajectory of s_t is governed by a first order Markov chain with two states so that the transition probability from state i to state j is

$$P(s_t = j | s_{t-1} = i) = p_{ij}, \quad i, j = 1, 2. \tag{3.19}$$

Because there are only two regimes, the corresponding matrix of transition probabilities is written thus:

$$\mathrm{M} = \begin{pmatrix} p_{11} & 1 - p_{11} \\ 1 - p_{22} & p_{22} \end{pmatrix}.$$

The next stage requires the estimation of the vector of the parameters $\theta = (c_1, c_2, \phi, p_{11}, p_{22}, \sigma^2)$, which most frequently is achieved by maximum likelihood. When this is done, the cycle in question is associated to a binary variable ξ_t, which takes a value of 1 during expansions and 0 during contractions. To construct ξ_t, one needs to adopt a rule comparing the probability of being in expansion with a critical value (equal to 0.5 in Hamilton). So, if $P(s_t = 1 | \Omega_k = \{y_k\}_{k-1}^t \geq 0.5$, ξ_t is positioned equal to one and the economy is expanding; it retracts when this probability is inferior to ½.

The model can be made more complex if we envisage more than two regimes, or even by making the transition probabilities dependent on the length of expansion and contraction phases. The essence of the method would still be expressed by the model (3.18)–(3.19).

Now let us consider a column vector $\mathbf{y}_t$ which consists of n time series, meant to represent global economic activity. Automating the selection procedure of the turning points common to these series requires leaving the subjectivity of the NBER's choices. To this end, Pagan and Harding (2006a, b, p. 75 et sq.) have perfected a non-parametric algorithm of extraction from the common cycle. Without going into too many details, we can say that the heart of the procedure comes from the evaluation of a characteristic of proximity for the clusters of turning points. The algorithm, although calibrated on Australian data, is able to closely reproduce the dating of the reference cycle by the NBER.

Alternatively, many authors base themselves on a model to determine a given cycle with the series $y_{jt}, j = 1, \ldots, n$. The process used is easily expressed, it simply uses the representation

$$\Delta y_{jt} = \alpha \Delta f_t + \varepsilon_{jt}, \tag{3.20}$$

where f_t is a common component to the whole series—it can be similar to a index of coincident indicators—and ε_{jt} is a random term specific to each j series. Of course, several hypotheses can be constructed on Δf_t, and ε_{jt}, which would result in as many different models. Stock and Watson's (1991), quoted above, is one example. Forni et al. (2001) are based on a generalised dynamic factor model (GDFM) to construct a synthetic coincident indicator for the Eurozone. Chauvet (1998), on the other hand, combines a GDFM with a Markovian regime-switching model, which results in a chronology of the American cycle very similar to the NBER's.

References

Abramovitz, M. (1961). The nature and significance of Kuznets cycles. *Economic Development and Cultural Change, 9*, 225–248.

Baxter, M., & King, R. G. (1999). Measuring business cycles: Approximate band-pass filters for economic time series. *Review of Economics and Statistics, 85*, 575–593.

Beveridge, S., & Nelson, C. (1981). A new approach to decomposition of economic time series into permanent and transitory components with particular attention to measurement of the business cycle. *Journal of Monetary Economics, 7*, 151–174.

Bismans, F., & Mougeot, C. (2008). La théorie autrichienne du cycle économique: un test économétrique. *Revue française d'économie, 22*, 73–102.

Boschan, C., & Ebanks, W. W. (1978). The phase-average trend: A new way of measuring growth. In *Proceedings of the Business and Economic Statistics Section* (pp. 332–335). American Statistical Association.

Box, G. E. P., & Jenkins, G. M. (1970). *Time series analysis: Forecasting and control.* San Francisco: Holden-Day.

Bry, G., & Boschan, C. (1971). *Cyclical analysis of time series: Selected procedures and computer programs*, Technical Paper 20. New York: National Bureau of Economic Research.

Burns, A. F., & Mitchell, W. C. (1946). *Measuring business cycles.* New York: National Bureau of Economic Research.

Campbell, J. Y., & Mankiw, N. G. (1987). Permanent and transitory components in macroeconomic fluctuations. *American Economic Review, 77*, 111–117.

Chauvet, M. (1998). An econometric characterization of business cycle dynamics with factor structure and Markov switching. *International Economic Review, 39*, 969–996.

Christiano, L., & Fitzgerald, T. (2003). The band pass filter. *International Economic Review, 44*, 435–465.

Cogley, T. (2006). Data filters, article écrit pour le. In *The new Palgrave dictionary of economics* (p. 10).

Cooley, T. F., & Le Roy, S. F. (1985). Atheoretical macroeconomics. *Journal of Monetary Economics, 16*, 283–308.

Cwik, P. (1998). The recession of 1990: A comment. *The Quarterly Journal of Austrian Economics, 1*, 85–88.

De Jong, D. N., & Dave, C. (2007). *Structural macroeconometrics*. Princeton-Oxford: Princeton University Press.

Dickey, D., & Fuller, W. (1979). Distribution of the estimators for autoregressive time series with a unit root. *Journal of the American Statistical Association, 74*, 427–431.

Dickey, D., & Fuller, W. (1981). Likelihood ratio statistics for autoregressive time series with a unit root. *Econometrica, 49*, 1057–1072.

Diebolt, C. (2005). Long cycles revisited. An essay in econometric history. *Economies et Sociétés, Série AF: Histoire Economique Quantitative, 32*, 23–47.

Ferrara, L. (2009). Caractérisation et datation des cycles économiques en zone euro. *Revue économique, 60*, 703–712.

Forni, M., Hallin, M., Lippi, M., & Reichlin, L. (2000). The generalized dynamic-factor model: Identification and estimation. *Review of Economics and Statistics, 82*, 540–554.

Forni, M., Hallin, M., Lippi, M., & Reichlin, L. (2001). Coincident and leading indicators for the euro area. *Economic Journal, 111*, C62–C85.

Freeman, C. (Ed.). (1996). *Long wave theory*. Cheltenham: E. Elgar.

Fuller, W. A. (1976). *Introduction to statistical time series*. New York: Wiley.

Garrison, R. W. (1986). Hayekian trade cycle theory: A reappraisal. *Cato Journal, 6*, 437–459.

Garrison, R. W. (1989). The Austrian theory of the business cycle in the light of modern macroeconomics. *The Review of Austrian Economics, 2*, 3–29.

Garrison, R. W. (1997). Austrian theory of business cycles. In D. Glasner (Ed.), *Business cycles and depressions: An encyclopaedia* (pp. 23–27). New York and London: Garland Publishing, INC.

Garrison, R. W. (2001). *Time and money. The macroeconomics of capital structure*. London-New York: Routledge.

Gordon, D., Weisskopf, T., & Bowles, S. (1983). Long swings and the nonreproductive cycle. *American Economic Review, 73*, 152–157.

Granger, C., & Newbold, P. (1974). Spurious regressions in econometrics. *Journal of Econometrics, 2*, 111–120.

Hamilton, J. D. (1989). A new approach to the economic analysis of nonstationary time series and the business cycle. *Econometrica, 57*, 357–384.

Harding, D., & Pagan, A. (2002). Dissecting the cycle: A methodological investigation. *Journal of Monetary Economics, 49*, 365–381.

Harding, D., & Pagan, A. (2006a). *Measurement of business cycles* (Vol. 966, p. 12), *Research Paper*. University of Melbourne.

Harding, D., & Pagan, A. (2006b). Synchronisation of cycles. *Journal of Econometrics, 132*, 59–79.

Harvey, A. (1989). *Forecasting, structural time series models and the Kalman filter*. Cambridge: Cambridge University Press.

Hayek, F. A. (1928). Equilibre intertemporel de prix et mouvements de valeur de la monnaie. *Revue française d'économie, 6*(1992), 105–149.

Hayek, F. A. (1974). The pretence of knowledge. In F. A. Hayek (1978b) *New studies in philosophy, politics, economics and the history of ideas* (pp. 23–34). London: Routledge and Kegan.
Hodrick, R., & Prescott, E. (1997). Postwar U.S. business cycles: An empirical investigation. *Journal of Money, Credit and Banking, 29*, 1–16.
Hughes, A. M. (1997). The recession of 1990: An Austrian explanation. *The Review of Austrian Economics, 10*, 23–40.
Imbert, G. (1959). *Des mouvements de longue durée Kondratieff*. Aix-en-Provence: La pensée universitaire.
Juglar, C. (1862). *Des crises commerciales et de leur retour périodique en France, en Angleterre et aux Etats-Unis*. Paris: Guillaumin et Cie.
Keeler, J. P. (2001). Empirical evidence on the Austrian business cycle theory. *The Review of Austrian Economics, 14*, 331–351.
Kirzner, I. (1973). *Competition and entrepreneurship*. Chicago: University of Chicago Press.
Kirzner, I. (1979). *Perception, opportunity and profit: Studies in the theory of entrepreneurship*. Chicago: University of Chicago Press.
Kleinknecht, A. (1987). *Innovation patterns in crisis and prosperity: Schumpeter's long cycle reconsidered*. London: The Macmillan Press Ltd.
Kresge, S., & Wenar, L. (1994). *Hayek on Hayek. An autobiographical dialogue*. Chicago: The University of Chicago Press.
Kuznets, S. (1930). *Secular movements in production and prices. Their nature and their bearing upon cyclical fluctuation*. Boston: Houghton Mifflin Co.
Kydland, F., & Prescott, E. (1982). Time to build and aggregate fluctuations. *Econometrica, 50* (1982), 1345–1370.
Long, J., & Plosser, C. (1983). Real business cycle. *Journal of Political Economy, 91*, 39–69.
Lucas, R. (1976). Econometric policy evaluation: A critique. In K. Brunner & A. Meltzern (Eds.), *The Phillips curve and labormarkets* (pp. 19–46). Amsterdam: North Holland. Carnegie-Rochester conference series on public policy 1.
Lumsdaine, R. L., & Papell, D. H. (1997). Multiple trend breaks and the unit root hypothesis. *Review of Economics and Statistics, 79*, 212–218.
Mensch, G. (1977). *Das technologische Patt. Innovationen überwinden die Depression*. Frankfurt am Main: Fischer Taschenbuch Verlag.
Minsky, H. P. (1957). Monetary systems and accelerator models. *American Economic Review, 47*, 860–883.
Minsky, H. P. (1975). *John Maynard Keynes*. New York: McGraw-Hill, 2008.
Minsky, H. P. (1986). *Stabilizing an unstable economy*. Mc Graw-Hill, 2008.
Mulligan, R. (2002). An Hayekian analysis of the term structure of production. *The Quarterly Journal of Austrian Economics, 5*, 17–33.
Mulligan, R. (2006). An empirical examination of Austrian business cycles theory. *The Quarterly Journal of Austrian Economics, 9*, 69–93.
NBER. (2009). *Business cycles expansions and contractions*. Available on http://www.nber.org/cycles.html.
Nelson, C. R. (1972). The prediction performance of the FRB-MIT-PENN model of the U.S. economy. *American Economic Review, 62*, 902–917.
Nelson, C. R., & Plosser, C. I. (1982). Trends and random walks in macroeconomic time series. *Journal of Monetary Economics, 10*, 139–162.
O'Driscoll, G., & Shenoy, S. R. (1976). Inflation, recession and stagflation. In E. G. Dolan (Ed.), *The foundations of modern Austrian economics* (pp. 185–211). Kansas City: Sheed and Ward.
Patinkin, D. (1956). *Money, interest and prices: An integration of monetary and value theory*. Evanston: Row Peterson.
Perron, P. (1988). Trends and random walks in macroeconomic time series: Further evidence from a new approach. *Journal of Economic Dynamics and Control, 12*, 297–332.
Perron, P. (1989). The great crash, the oil price shock and the unit root hypothesis. *Econometrica, 57*, 1361–1401.

Persons, W. M. (1919). Indices of business conditions. *Review of Economic Statistics, 1*, 5–110.

Plosser, C. I. (1989). Understanding real business cycles. *Journal of Economic Perspectives, 3*, 51–78.

Powell, B. (2002). Explaining Japan's recession. *The Quarterly Journal of Austrian Economics, 5*, 35–50.

Romer, C. D. (1994). Remeasuring business cycles. *The Journal of Economic History, 54*, 573–609.

Rothbard, M. (1975). *America's great depression*. Kansas City: Sheed and Ward.

Samuelson, P. A. (1939). Interactions between the multiplier analysis and the principle of acceleration. *Review of Economic Statistics, 21*, 75–78.

Samuelson, P. A. (1948). *Foundations of economic analysis*. Harvard University Press.

Samuelson, P. A., & Solow, R. M. (1960). Analytical aspects of anti-inflation policy. *American Economic Review, 50*, 177–194.

Schumpeter, J. (1939). *Business cycles: A theoretical, historical and statistical analysis of the capitalist process* (Vol. 2). London: McGraw-Hill Book Co.

Sims, C. A. (Ed.). (1977). *New methods in business cycle research: Proceedings from a conference*. Federal Reserve Bank of Minneapolis.

Sims, C. (1980a). Macroeconomics and reality. *Econometrica, 48*, 1–48.

Sims, C. (1980b). Comparison of interwar and postwar cycles: Monetarism reconsidered. *American Economic Review, 70*, 250–257.

Stock, J. H., & Watson, M. W. (1991). A probabilistic model of coincident economic indicators. In K. Lahiri & G. H. Moore (Eds.), *Leading economic indicators: New approaches and forecasting records* (pp. 63–90). Cambridge: Cambridge University Press.

Weinstock, U. (1964). *Das problem der Kondratieff-Zyklen. Ein Beitrag zur Entwicklung einer Theorie der "langen Wellen" und ihrer Bedeutung*. Berlin: Duncker and Humblot.

Zivot, E., & Andrews, D. W. K. (1992). Further evidence on the great crash, the oil price shock and the unit root hypothesis. *Journal of Business and Economic Statistics, 10*, 251–270.

Chapter 4
Dating

Abstract This chapter is focused on the dating of the classical business cycle. It develops the relevant methodology, explains the regime switching models, presents the estimation technics and the associated tests, and finally offers applications to the dating of the French cycle and a Markov-switching model to the South African economy.

Keywords Business cycles · Dating · Econometrics · France · Markov-switching · Methodology · South Africa · Time series analysis

All the economies experience fluctuations in their level of activity as measured by Gross Domestic Product (GDP). Classically, a recession is defined by Burns and Mitchell (1946, p. 3) as a marked decline in the economic activity impacting its different sectors. A more modern definition, but identical in substance, is given by the American NBER: it's a period with "a significant decline in activity spread across the economy and lasting from a few months to more than a year." Similarly, in an expansion period, activity rises significantly, spread across the economy, and lasts several years.

This definition is that of the classical business cycle. From a formal viewpoint, if $y_t = \ln(Y_t)$ is the series of the real GDP in natural logarithm, the problem this perspective is to determine the turning points of y_t. However, there exists another approach of the fluctuations: that which studies the growth cycle—a concept defined by Mintz (1969); in this conception, the turning points are selected in the detrended series y_t—see also see e.g. Bismans and Majetti (2012) for some precisions.

This chapter has benefited from a significant contribution by Zohra Rabah.

T. Aimar et al., *Business Cycles in the Run of History*,
SpringerBriefs in Economics, DOI 10.1007/978-3-319-24325-2_4

This chapter is exclusively focused on the dating of the classical business cycle. To this effect, two great procedures are relevant: non parametric algorithms and parametric models based on regime-switching. These latter constructs are widely used to detect cycles in various economies: see e.g. Hamilton (1989), Goodwin (1993), Krolzig (1997), Chauvet (1998), Kim and Nelson (1999a, b), Kaufmann (2000), Kontolemis (2001), Chauvet and Hamilton (2006), Caraiani (2010), Damette and Rabah (2010).

Our chapter is structured as following. Section 4.1 develops the relevant methodology. It explains the two types of regime switching models used by the authors. It also presents the estimation technics and the associated tests. The subsequent section is devoted to the dating of the French cycle. Finally, Markov-switching model is applied to the South African economy.

4.1 Methodology

It exists several kinds of regime switching models—see Teräsvirta (2006) on the subject—, e.g. Self-exciting Threshold Autoregressions (SETAR), Smooth Transition Autoregressions (STAR) or logistic STAR (LSTAR) and Markov-switching models (MS). Only these latter are used in this chapter.

4.1.1 Markov-Switching Models

Two types of models must be distinguished: Markov-switching autoregressions (MS-AR) and Markov-switching Dynamic regressions (MS-DR).

Introduce firstly the MS-AR models and consider two regimes denoted by $s_t = 0$ if the economy is in recession and $s_t = 1$ if it is in an expansion phase. This variable is unobservable, but it is supposed to follow a finite Markov chain. The probability of moving from regime *i* to regime *j* is defined by

$$p_{j\,|\,i} = P(s_{t+1} = j | s_t = i), \quad i,j = 0,1. \tag{4.1}$$

The conditional probabilities in (4.1) are temporally constant. However, we have the constraint that $\sum_{j=0}^{1} p_{j\,|\,i} = 1$.

As viewed in Chap. 3 of this book, the matrix of transition probabilities is written as follows:

$$\mathbf{P} = \left(\begin{array}{c|cc|c} & s_{t+1} = 0 & s_{t+1} = 1 & \text{Sum} \\ \hline s_t = 0 & p_{0|0} & p_{1|0} & 1 \\ s_t = 1 & p_{0|1} & p_{1|1} & 1 \end{array} \right)$$

After, the hypothesis is made that the mean of the autoregressive process depends of regimes following the scheme:

$$\mu(s_t) = \begin{cases} \mu(0) \text{ if } s_t = 0 \\ \mu(1) \text{ if } s_t = 1. \end{cases} \tag{4.2}$$

The MS-AR(2, p) model can then be written as

$$y_t = \mu(s_t) + \sum_{i=1}^{p} \rho_i (y_{t-i} - \mu(s_{t-i})) + \varepsilon_t, \quad \varepsilon_t \sim N(0, \sigma^2), \quad t = 1, \cdots, T \tag{4.3}$$

As far as the Markov-switching Dynamic Regression model is concerned, it includes in addition of (4.3) a vector of K explanatory variables so that its general formulation is the following:

$$y_t = \mu(s_t) + \sum_{i=1}^{p} \rho_i y_{t-i} + \mathbf{x}_t' \boldsymbol{\beta} + \varepsilon_t, \quad \varepsilon_t \sim N(0, \sigma^2), \quad t = 1, \cdots, T. \tag{4.4}$$

The vector $\boldsymbol{\beta}$ is of course a column vector of the K parameters of the regression.

4.1.2 Estimation

The estimation of (4.3) is involved, because there are 2^{1+p} different regimes and thus it is necessary to estimate a state vector with 2^{1+p} components. As a result, the problem is intractable when the model uses monthly data. The MS-DR process is easier to estimate, given that the number of states is equal to the number of regimes, namely two in the current case.

Consequently, for the sake of simplicity, consider first an MS-DR (2,1) model:

$$y_t = \mu(S_t) + \phi y_{t-1} + \mathbf{x}_t' \boldsymbol{\beta} + \varepsilon_t, \quad \varepsilon_t \sim N(0, \sigma^2), \quad t = 1, \cdots, T. \tag{4.5}$$

Let $Y_t = (y_t, y_{t-1}, \cdots, y_1)$ the vector compounding by all the observations through date t. Denote by $\boldsymbol{\theta} = \left(\mu(0), \mu(1), \phi, \boldsymbol{\beta}, p_{0|0}, p_{1|1}\right)$ the vector of the parameters in (4.5). The density of y_t is conditional on $S_t = \{0, 1\}$, so that

$$f(y_t | S_t = j, Y_{t-1}; \boldsymbol{\theta}) = (1/\sigma\sqrt{2\pi}) e^{-(1/2\sigma^2)(y_t - \mu(S_t) - \phi y_{t-1} - \mathbf{x}_t' \boldsymbol{\beta})^2} \tag{4.6}$$

Two algorithms are available, which yield as a by-product the likelihood or log-likelihood function: the filtering as well smoothing of regime probabilities. Focus will fall on filtering, as it can be used more directly that the second algorithm.

The filter developed by Hamilton (1989), but based on Cosslett and Lee (1985), is similar in spirit to the Kalman filter conceived for the linear state-space models. The filter permits drawing forecasts of the unobserved regime. The regime forecasts conditioned by the information available up to time t are referred to as *filtered probabilities*, $P(s_t = j | Y_t, \boldsymbol{\theta})$. For $j = 0, 1$, and each time t, the prediction and *filtering* probabilities of the regime $s_t = j$, are obtained by iterating on the following equations:

$$P(s_t = j|Y_{t-1}; \boldsymbol{\theta}) = P(s_t = j|s_{t-1} = i, Y_{t-1}; \boldsymbol{\theta})P(s_{t-1} = j|Y_{t-1}; \boldsymbol{\theta}), \quad (4.7)$$

$$P(s_t = j|Y_t; \boldsymbol{\theta}) = \frac{f(y_t|s_t = j, Y_{t-1}; \boldsymbol{\theta})P(s_t = j|Y_{t-1}; \boldsymbol{\theta})}{f(y_t|Y_{t-1}; \boldsymbol{\theta})}, \quad (4.8)$$

where $P(S_{t+1} = i|S_t = j, Y_t; \boldsymbol{\theta})$ is the transition probability. Moreover, $f(y_t|Y_{t-1}; \boldsymbol{\theta}) = \sum_{j=0}^{1} f(y_t|s_t = j, Y_{t-1}; \boldsymbol{\theta})P(s_t = j|Y_{t-1}; \boldsymbol{\theta})$ is the density of y_t conditional on Y_{t-1} alone. Given a starting value for the probability $P(s_0 = j|Y_0; \boldsymbol{\theta})$, we can then iterate the Eqs. (4.7) and (4.8) for $t = 1, 2, \ldots, T$ to get the *filtering probabilities* $P(s_t = j|Y_t; \boldsymbol{\theta})$.

As the density of y_t is computed conditional to its past at each t by the filter, the likelihood function is

$$\ln L(\boldsymbol{\theta}) = \ln \prod_{t=1}^{T} f(y_t|Y_{t-1}; \boldsymbol{\theta}). \quad (4.9)$$

The log-likelihood which is a function of $\boldsymbol{\theta}$, but also of the transition probabilities $p_{j|i}$, is maximized subject to the twofold constraint that these probabilities lie between 0 and 1 and their sum equals one. It remains then to employ an algorithm such as that of Dempster et al. (1977) to solve this optimization program.

Now, consider an MS-AR(2,p) model given as follows:

$$y_t = \mu(s_t) + \phi(y_{t-1}) - \mu(s_{t-1}) + \varepsilon_t, \quad \varepsilon_t \sim N(0, \sigma^2), \quad t = 1, \cdots, T \quad (4.10)$$

The underlying unknown parameters, that describe the model in (4.10), consist of the two mean parameters μ_1 and μ_2, the variance σ, the autoregressive component ϕ, and the transition probabilities $p_{j|i}$. These parameters can be collected in a vector $\boldsymbol{\theta}$. As the mean is switching in (4.10), the density of y_t is conditional on the last $2^{(2)}$ regime realizations, such that

$$f(y_t|S_t = j, S_{t-1} = i, Y_{t-1}; \boldsymbol{\theta}) = 1/\sigma\sqrt{2\pi}\, e^{-1/(2\sigma^2)[(y_t-\mu(s_t))-\varphi(y_{t-1}-\mu(s_{t-1}))]^2}. \quad (4.11)$$

The density of y_t is then a mixture of four Gaussian distributions corresponding to each of the four regimes. As for the MS-DR(2,1), the associated likelihood function as given in (4.9) can be computed as by-product of the nonlinear Hamilton's (1989) filter, from which the Maximum Likelihood Estimates (MLE) can be found. Again, the *filtering* probabilities of $S_t = j$ can be obtained by iterating on the Eqs. (4.7) and (4.8) and summing $P(S_t = j, S_{t-1} = i|Y_t; \boldsymbol{\theta})$ over all values of $S_{t-1} = i$ as follows:

$$P(S_t = j|Y_t; \boldsymbol{\theta}) = \sum_{i=0}^{1} P(S_t = j, S_{t-1} = i|Y_t; \boldsymbol{\theta}). \quad (4.12)$$

These probabilities provide information on the regime at every point in time, being useful tools for dating regime switches.

Estimates of the unobserved regime at every period t using the full-sample information can be also be used. To compute such smoothing estimates for $P(S_t = j|Y_T; \boldsymbol{\theta})$, we implement the Kim's (1994) smoother. For $i, j = 0, 1$, the smoothing probabilities are obtained as follows:

$$P(S_t = j|Y_T; \boldsymbol{\theta}) = \sum_{i=0}^{1} P(S_{t+1} = i|Y_T; \boldsymbol{\theta}) P(S_t = j|S_{t+1} = i, Y_t; \boldsymbol{\theta}), \tag{4.13}$$

where

$$P(S_t = j|S_{t+1} = i, Y_t; \boldsymbol{\theta}) = \frac{P(S_t = j|Y_t; \boldsymbol{\theta}) P(S_{t+1} = i|S_t = j, Y_t; \theta)}{P(S_{t+1} = i|Y_t; \boldsymbol{\theta})}. \tag{4.14}$$

Given a starting value of $P(S_T = j|Y_T; \boldsymbol{\theta})$ by the filtering algorithm, one can iterate on the Eqs. (4.13) and (4.14) for $t = T-1, T-2, \ldots, 1$, to draw easily the smoothing probabilities $P(S_t = j|Y_T; \boldsymbol{\theta})$.

4.1.3 Testing for Nonlinearity

The MS model is intrinsically non-linear. However, devising a test for nonlinearity is not an easy task, because a MS model nests a linear model and is not identified, under the null, if linearity is verified.

Formal testing for nonlinearity with Markov-switching models is hindered by the presence of nuisance parameters that are only identified under the alternative hypothesis and by the problem of singular information matrix at the null hypothesis (See Teräsvirta (2006) for a synthesis). For example, testing problem in (4.9) amounts to decide between a linear model with constant parameters, such that $\mu_0 = \mu_1$, and a nonlinear model with switching parameters, that is $\mu_0 \neq \mu_1$. Under the null hypothesis, the transition probabilities $p_{0|0}$ and $p_{1|1}$ are no longer identified. They can take any value without varying the likelihood function. Moreover, the scores with respect to $(\mu_0 - \mu_1)$, $p_{0|0}$, and $p_{1|1}$ are identically zero at the null, thereby leading to the degeneracy of the information matrix. It follows that the standard likelihood-based tests will no longer have standard asymptotic distributions.

Davies (1977) was the first to cope with the problem of unidentified nuisance parameters under the null. Hansen (1992) developed the solution in the framework of MS models. He then provided a bound for the asymptotic distribution of the supremum of a Likelihood ratio statistic in the setting of unidentified nuisance parameters and singular information matrix. The bound is model and data dependent, which makes the tabulation of critical value impossible. The empirical distribution can be determined through Monte Carlo simulations. However, the lower bound yields conservative critical values, causing an under-rejection of the null when it is true.

Later, Garcia (1998) reviewed the testing problem in Hansen (1992) and, derived an asymptotic null distribution for the supremum of the LR test statistic. He proceeded as the change in Markov-switching parameters $(\mu_0 - \mu_1)$ is identified under the null. Then, by restricting the values of the transition probabilities away from zero and one, he considered that the problem of identically null score no longer exists. He provided asymptotic critical values for some Markov-switching models, which only depend on model specification. As Garcia (1998) does not account for the zero scores problem under the null, the validity of the asymptotic distribution of his test may be questioned. Gong and Mariano (1997) viewed that the Garcia's asymptotic distribution is not the exact distribution but an approximation which is found to be close to the empirical distribution.

Recently, Carrasco et al. (2014) developed an information-matrix-based test which only requires the estimation of the model under the null. To compute the critical values, the test requires bootstrap parametric simulations. Bootstrap procedures provide an alternative way to approximate the unknown true distribution. In the setting of unidentified nuisance parameters, the test statistic is not asymptotically *pivotal*. For example, under nonstandard setting, a LR statistic is no longer distributed as chi-square distribution. It is unclear what the unknown distribution of the LR test statistic is or whether it is *pivotal*. Meanwhile, bootstrap tests are found to perform well, even in the presence of unidentified nuisance parameters. Di Sanzo (2009) have shown that a related semi-parametric bootstrap LR test has much higher power than the Carrasco et al.'s and Hansen's test for some Markov-switching models. Morley and Rabah (2014) employed Monte Carlo analysis to consider small sample properties of the Carrasco et al.'s test and found that it has very little power to detect a Markov-switching in mean or intercept of an autoregressive process when taking serial correlation into account under the linear null hypothesis. By contrast, a parametric bootstrap LR test retains a considerable power in this setting. Given these results, we bootstrap the distribution of the LR statistic to detect nonlinearity for the MS-AR(2,*p*) model discussed above.

4.2 Dating the French Business Cycle

In the aftermath of the Great Recession, a renewed interest in the role of nonlinearity in reproducing business-cycle fluctuations has been sparked among economists and statisticians, providing them an opportunity to re-assess its importance. Meanwhile, the literature examining the presence of Markov-switching regimes or of potential nonlinearities in French data is considerably scarce, being limited to work of Rabault (1993), Damette and Rabah (2010), and Bec et al. (2015). Therefore, a new application using recent data or a new form of MS models seems to be useful to identify recent stylized facts of business cycles which can help in directing choices over time series modelling.

To this extent, we explore the reliability of two variants of MS models of real GDP growth to capture classical business cycle phases of "expansion" and "recession" in France for the period 1976–2014.

4.2.1 Data and Models

We follow the subsequent literature and use natural logarithms of real GDP, y_t, to investigate the French business cycle. Our data are quarterly real GDP downloaded from the Insee (National Institute for Statistics and Economic Studies) database. The sample period ranges from the first quarter of 1976 to the third quarter of 2014. The 1976Q1 start date for the sample period is designed to avoid the presence of a structural break in mean.

An investigation of the historical record of France's economy shows that France experienced a period of strong growth during the thirty glorious years, which petered out in the early 1970s with the first oil shock. The evidence for a reduction in mean of the real GDP growth rate has been documented in Damette and Rabah (2010) and Bec et al. (2015). Moreover, several studies has pointed out the sensitivity of MS models to the presence of structural breaks for the U.S. economy (e.g., Kim and Nelson 1999b, McConnell and Perez-Quiros 2000, and Perron and Wada 2009) and for France (e.g., Damette and Rabah 2010). Thus, we consider only post-break observations, starting from 1976Q1.

Following standard practice in the literature, we consider estimated seasonally adjusted data, assuming that seasonal patterns and business cycles are not correlated.

To better capture regimes changes in French real GDP, we use both MS specifications discussed in Sect. 4.2 [i.e. MS-AR(2,p) and MS-DR(2,p)].

The MS-AR model given in (4.3) is the original demeaned specification of Hamilton (1989) with two states, when only the mean $\mu(s_t)$ depends on the state s_t. To remove non stationarity, we estimate the model on Δy_t measured as 100 times the first differences of the natural logarithms of the level of GDP, which is also the quarterly French growth rate, and μ_{S_t} measures its regime-dependent long-run mean. The MS-AR(2,p) given in (4.3) can be rewritten as:

$$\Delta y_t = \mu(s_t) + \sum_{i=1}^{p} \rho_i(\Delta y_{t-i} - \mu(s_{t-i})) + \varepsilon_t, \quad \varepsilon_t \sim N(0, \sigma^2), \quad t = 1, \cdots, T.$$

Hence, μ_0 is the mean growth rate characterizing a low growth state and μ_1 is that of a high growth state. When the economic activity switches from $s_t = 0$ to $s_t = 1$, the GDP growth rate switches from μ_0 to μ_1. We conduct Maximum Likelihood Estimation (MLE) to estimate the MS-AR model and use the Akaike Information Criterion (AIC) to select the lag length p. We find that the preferred model is an MS-AR(2,2) model. Note that a problem of numerous local optima arises in estimation. To address this problem, we try different starting values and choose the local maximum that has the largest value of the likelihood function.

Next, we consider the MS-DR(2,p) model as given in (4.4) for the log of quarterly French real GDP, y_t. The set of regressors in the vector $\mathbf{x}_t$ are:

- the monetary aggregate M1;
- the yield rate on the Government bonds with a maturity of ten years, hereafter denoted by Gbond10;
- the yield on three-month Treasury bills, denoted Tbill3;
- the interest rate spread denoted by SPREAD and defined as the difference between the interest rate on government bonds at 10 years (Gbond10) and that of treasury bills at 3 months (Tbill3);
- the Euro Dollar exchange rate.

To specify our MS-DR model, we apply the "general-to-specific" approach of Hendry (1993). We find that an MS-DR model with two states and an auto-regression of order one is the most suitable form.

To identify business cycle phases for both models, the smoothed probability $P(s_t = j|Y_T; \boldsymbol{\theta})$ is used. As already mentioned in Sect. 4.2, this probability is the estimated conditional probability of being in state j conditional on the full sample of growth rate observations, Y_T. The dating rule proposed by Hamilton (1989) is to compare the smoothed probability that the economy is in recession phase $P(s_t = 0|Y_t; \boldsymbol{\theta})$ to a critical value c, which is set equal to 0.5. When this probability is greater than 0.5, a recession is signaled (i.e. $s_t = 0$). Inversely, when $P(s_t = 0|Y_t; \boldsymbol{\theta}) \leq 0.5$ that is equivalent to $P(s_t = 1|Y_t; \boldsymbol{\theta}) > 0.5$, the economy is expanding (i.e., $s_t = 1$).

Hence, a peak at t which marks the end of an expansion at t is detected if the smoothed probability switches from beyond 0.5 to above 0.5 at $t + 1$. The peak date is then the period t just before the start of a recession phase. Also, a trough at t is located if the economy is in recession at t, i.e., $P(S_t = 0|Y_t; \boldsymbol{\theta}) > 0.5$, and this smoothed probability moves beyond 0.5 at $t + 1$.

4.2.2 Estimation and Results (I)

The MS-AR specification is first applied to the quarterly real GDP series for the period 1976Q1-2014Q2. Thus, let 1976Q1 correspond to the first observation of French data to estimate the parameters of the models or failing that, the first quarter available since three quarters (for MS-AR(2,2)) are allowed for detrending and lags.

Since there is no reference business cycle chronology for France, it is difficult to verify the dates of the turning points potentially identified by every research dedicated to the French business cycle. For that reason, we take the turning point chronology derived from a non-parametric approach, namely the quarterly version of the Bry and Boschan's (1971) algorithm (BBQ), as it is accurately located.

We thus compare the resulting turning point chronologies to that derived by the BBQ algorithm.

The estimated parameters of the MS-AR(2,2) model are reported in Table 4.1.

A prominent fact from Table 4.1 is the significance of the autoregressive parameters, supporting the AIC results. Our estimates also provide a negative growth rate is of −0.907 during recessions and a positive growth rate of 0.489 during expansions. The recession's growth rate is not significantly different from zero. In terms of probabilities, the results indicate that the probability of remaining in an expansion phase is of 0.987, whereas the probability of staying in a recession period is only of 0.366. The latter is not significantly different from zero. Given these probabilities, an expansion phase has an expected duration of $1/(1-p_{1|1}) \simeq 76.92$ quarters and an average recession phase lasts $1/(1-p_{0|0}) \simeq 1.57$ quarter.

Recessions are determined from the MS-AR(2,2) model using the smoothed probabilities, which are plotted in Fig. 4.1. For the purpose of comparison, the recession periods as identified by the BBQ algorithm are represented by shaded grey areas in Fig. 4.1.

The outcome of applying the BBQ algorithm identifies three recessions during the period under investigation. It indicates that French economy has entered into a recession in the second quarter of 1980, and exited it in the fourth quarter of 1980. Then after an expansion period, France fell back into a recession in the second quarter of 1992—associated to the collapse of the European Monetary System

Table 4.1 Maximum likelihood estimates from MS-AR(2,2) model

	μ_0	μ_1	ϕ_1	ϕ_2	σ	$p_{0\|0}$	$p_{1\|1}$
Estimates	−0.907	0.489	0.351	0.239	0.624	0.366	0.987
	(0.351)	(0.078)	(0.097)	(0.082)	(0.026)	(0.326)	(0.013)

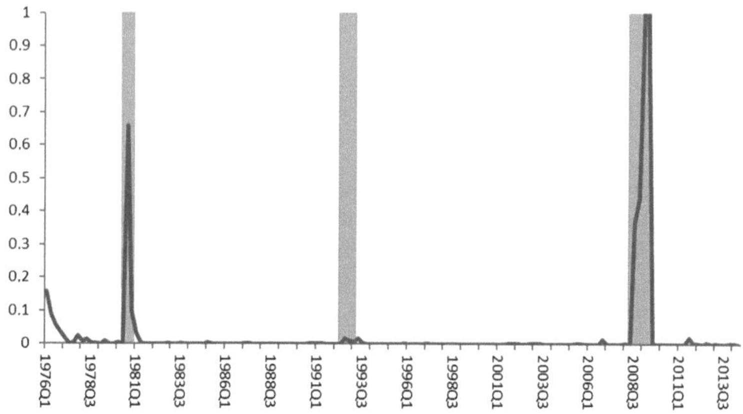

Fig. 4.1 Smoothed French recession probabilities obtained from MS-AR(2,2). *Note* The *grey shaded areas* indicate the French recessions as identified by the BBQ algorithm

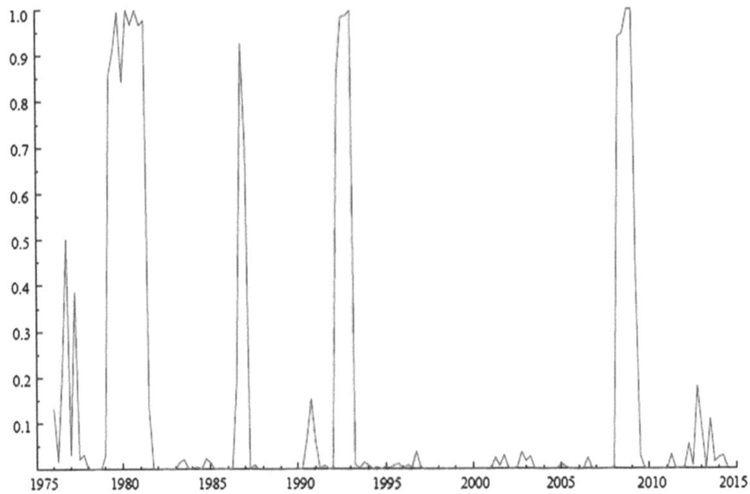

Fig. 4.2 The smoothed probabilities of recession resulting from the MS-DR(2,1) model

(EMS) in the aftermath of German reunification—and emerged from it in the second quarter of 1993, after having bottomed at the identified GDP trough in the first quarter of 1993. The French economy has entered a new recession—sparked the subprime crisis—in the second quarter of 2008 until the second quarter of 2009.

From Fig. 4.1, two out of three recession periods are determined with smoothed probability greater than 0.5: the first one with a peak in the second quarter of 1980 and trough in the third quarter of 1980, and the second one with the peak in the fourth quarter of 2008 and trough in the second quarter of 2009. As is clearly evident from Fig. 4.2, the chronology obtained from the MS-AR(2,2) model does not correspond to the peak and trough dates resulting from the BBQ algorithm. The model misses the recession of the early 1990s.

4.2.3 Estimations and Results (II)

Table 4.2 summarizes the results from estimating the MS-DR(2,1) model.

As is obvious from Table 4.2, all of the estimates are significantly different from zero. Also, the intercept estimate is different from one state to another: the intercept value during an recession phase is lower than that for an expansion phase. The transition probability estimates $p_{0|0}$ and $p_{1|1}$, imply that a recession phase has an expected duration of around two quarters and that an average expansion period lasts for around 21 quarters.

Figure 4.2 plots the smoothed probabilities of recession resulting from the MS-DR(2,1) model. As can be seen, three recessions are depicted: the first has occurred between 1979 and 1980; the second is of 1992/93; finally, the 2008/09

Table 4.2 Maximum likelihood estimates from MS-DR(2,1) model

	Estimates	Standard errors
μ_0	0.250	0.009
μ_1	0.259	0.010
ϕ_1	0.980	0.001
GB10	0.002	0.001
GB10(−1)	−0.003	0.001
TB3	0.002	0.000
TB3(−1)	−0.002	0.001
$p_{0\|0}$	0.502	0.101
$p_{1\|1}$	0.954	0.023

recession following the "subprime" crisis. The MS-DR(2,1) identifies two further periods of economic slowdown in 1976 and in 1986. The first period cannot be considered as a recession period since the smoothed probability is close, but not greater than 0.5. The second period located by the model lasts for two quarters (1986Q4-1987Q1).

All in all, the results obtained from both MS specifications provide evidence of nonlinear dynamics present in the French business cycle. In particular, multivariate MS models provide a substantial improvement over an univariate MS model for reproducing certain business-cycle fluctuations. These results are in a good agreement with those about nonlinearity testing. Applying a bootstrap LR test to French real GDP data produces a rejection of linearity at the 5 % conventional level. The LR test statistic takes a value of 12.05 and exceeds the bootstrap critical value of 8.92 at the 5 % significance level.

Based on these results, we conclude that there exists support for nonlinear Markov-switching dynamics in French real GDP.

4.3 The Case of South Africa

South African economy has deeply changed since the full democratisation of the country in 1994–1995. [For a simple and funny presentation, see Roux (2011).] Today it is one member of the BRICS with Brasil, Russia, India and China.

Furthermore, only the MS-DR model is used to date the business cycle. Others relevant papers using a Markov model to study South African business cycle are those of Moolman (2004), Altug and Bildirici (2010), Bosch and Ruch (2012), and Bismans and Le Roux (2013).

4.3.1 Model and Data

The general model MS-DR is written in the form:

$$y_t = \mu(S_t) + \sum_{i=1}^{p} \rho_i y_{t-i} + \mathbf{x}_t'\boldsymbol{\beta} + \varepsilon_t, \quad \varepsilon_t \sim N(0, \sigma^2), \quad t = 1, \cdots, T,$$

where y_t is the quarterly real GDP, S_t the variable denoting the regimes (0 for recessions, 1 for expansions), $\mathbf{x}_t'$ a row vector of K exogenous variables possibly including lagged values of these explanatory variables, and $\boldsymbol{\beta}$ the corresponding column vector of the K parameters of regression.

Several variables were considered as regressors in the vector $\mathbf{x}_t$:

- the real investment, denoted INVr, which is a component of the global demand;
- the monetary aggregates M1 and M2;
- the yield rate on the Government bonds with a maturity of ten years, hereafter denoted by Gbond10;
- the yield on three-month Treasury bills, denoted Tbill3;
- the interest rate spread denoted by SPREAD and defined as the difference between the interest rate on government bonds at 10 years (Gbond10) and that of treasury bills at 3 months (Tbill3).

All these chronological series derive from the database of the South African Reserve Bank. The sample period extends from the first quarter of 1981 to the fourth quarter of 2010. This temporal interval is sufficiently long to get valuable results from the viewpoint of statistical inference.

4.3.2 Estimation and Tests

To determine the final form of the model, the procedure vindicated by Hendry (1993) is applied, so that a MS-DR (2,1) model is yield.

Table 4.3 presents the estimates for the parameters including transition probabilities.

Table 4.3 Estimation of the MS-DR(2,1) model

	Coefficients	Standard errors	*P*-values
$\boldsymbol{\mu}(\mathbf{0})$	0.0396	0.0042	0.000
$\boldsymbol{\mu}(\mathbf{1})$	0.0542	0.0043	0.000
LGDPr (−1)	0.9973	0.0003	0.000
Gbond10	0.002	0.0006	0.000
Gbond10 (−1)	−0.0025	0.0006	0.000
P(0|0)	0.502	0.1726	0.004
P(0|1)	0.083	0.034	0.016

Some findings are contained in Table 4.3. First, as can be seen from the p-values, it is clear that all the estimated coefficients are significantly different from zero. Secondly, the constants which are linked to the two regimes are such that the mean under the recession phase is lower than in the case of expansions. Thirdly, the probability to remain in recession is lower than the probability to leave the state of expansion and to experience a recession.

In order to evaluate the model, several tests were conducted. In the first place, the test of ARCH (Autoregressive Conditional Heteroscedasticity) effects, conceived by Engle (1982), is applied. It is well-known that it tests at the first order the nullity of γ_1 in the equation of squared residuals:

$$\hat{u}_t^2 = \gamma_0 + \gamma_1 \hat{u}_{t-1}^2 + e_t.$$

If no ARCH effects are present, the fitted equation will yield a low determination coefficient R^2. Asymptotically, the statistic $T \cdot R^2$, where T denotes the sample size, has a chi-square or F-distribution. Here are the statistic and p-value for $F(1108)$:

$$\text{ARCH} = 5.2138\,[0,0244].$$

In conclusion, we accept the null of residuals homoscedasticity at a significance level of one percent.

Finally, the linearity Likelihood Ratio test gives a statistic equal to 37.123 associated to a p-value of 0.000. This p-value results from the conventional chi-square distribution with three degrees of freedom. Furthermore, the upper bound for the sup-statistic yields a p-value of 0.000. Consequently, in both cases the null hypothesis of linearity is rejected, which confirms the superiority of the Markov-switching model with respect to its linear corresponding model.

4.3.3 A Chronology of the Business Cycle

The filtered, not smoothed, probabilities are used to establish the timing of the business cycle. Recall that these probabilities give the probability of the state $S_t = j$ conditionally to the set of observations up to the date t. As usual, the Hamilton's rule was adopted: the economy is in a state of recession when $P(S_t = 0|\Omega_t) > 0.5$ and in an expansion phase, otherwise.

The observations in Fig. 4.3 reveal that since 1980, the South African economy has experienced four major recessions. The filtered probabilities are also high or nearly one in the first quarter of 1986, the fourth quarter of 1989 as well the third quarter of 1998. Based on the conventional definition, a recession must last for at least two quarters. Consequently inappropriate signals have been eliminated before stating the precise timing of cyclical fluctuations.

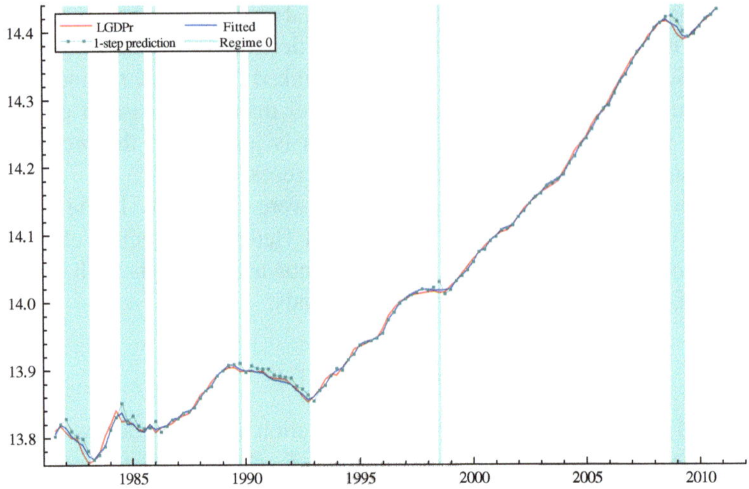

Fig. 4.3 Phases of recession

Table 4.4 Dating the South African classical business cycle

Recessions		Expansions	
Period	Duration	Period	Duration
1982Q1–1983Q1	6	1983Q2–1984Q2	5
1984Q3–1986Q1	5	1986Q2–1990Q4	19
1991Q1–1992Q4	8	1993Q1–2008Q3	63
2008Q4–2009Q3	4	2009Q4–...	

Table 4.4 shows the states of recessions and expansions, as identified from the application of the MS-DR, together with the durations in quarters of the various phases.

We first note that the duration of expansion phases is very moving. Especially remarkable is the long period of growth between 1993 and 2008. By comparison, the recessions are shorter. Finally, it is worthwhile to highlight an important aspect of South Africa's economic dynamics. As Laubscher (2004) has shown, the domestic business cycle is strongly impacted by the economic situation abroad. According to the NBER (2010) and Bismans and Majetti (2012), the US economy entered recession in the last quarter of 2007, while France, Germany, etc., followed in the second quarter of 2008. For its part, South Africa entered recession during the third quarter of 2008, as a direct consequence of the world contraction.

4.3.4 A Brief Comparison

As viewed sooner, two great sets of procedures are available to date fluctuations in economic activity: parametrical methods such that the use of Markov-switching models on a side; non parametrical approaches based on the detection of turning

Table 4.5 Turning points in the South African business cycle

Peaks		Troughs	
MS	BM	MS	BM
1981Q4	1981Q1	1983Q2	1983Q2
1984Q2	1984Q2	1986Q1	1986Q1
1990Q1	1989Q3	1992Q4	1992Q4
2008Q3	2008Q3	2009Q3	2009Q2

points in the GDP on the other side. At this end, various algorithms have been implemented. The most known is that of Bry and Boschan (1971), which has been notably transposed to quarterly series by Harding and Pagan (2002). For this reason, it is called BBQ algorithm. Bismans and Majetti (2012) have applied this algorithm to the South African GDP.

Thus a comparison between the two dating methods is useful, especially as the two chronologies measure the classical business cycle as it opposes to the growth cycle got by detrending. Table 4.5 gives the comparison between the chronology of this contribution (abbreviated as MS) and that of Bismans and Majetti (BM, 2012).

Clearly, the differences in the chronologies of turning points are extremely small. The only noteworthy gap is for the peak located in the first quarter of 1990 for MS procedure and in the third quarter of 1989 for Bismans-Majetti.

Proximity of dating demonstrates the merits of the Markov-switching modeling, a tool well-adapted to the research of turning points in economic activity.

References

Altug, S., & Bildirici, M. (2010). Business cycles around the world: A regime switching approach. Istanbul: Tüsiad-Koç University (Working Paper 1009).

Bec, F., Bouabdallah, O., & Ferrara, L. (2015). Comparing the shape of recoveries: France, the UK and the US. *Economic Modelling, 44*, 327–334.

Bismans, F., & Le Roux, P. (2013). Dating the business cycle in South Africa by using a Markov-switching model. *Journal for Studies in Economics and Econometrics, 37*, 25–39.

Bismans, F., & Majetti, R. (2012). Dating the South African business cycle. *Journal for Management and Leadership, 1*, 1–12.

Bosch, A., & Ruch, F. (2012). An alternative business cycle dating procedure for South Africa. South African Reserve Bank Working Paper, WP/12/06.

Bry, G., & Boschan, C. (1971). *Cyclical analysis of time series: Selected procedures and computer programs*. New York: National Bureau of Economic Research (Technical Paper 20).

Burns, A. F., & Mitchell, W. C. (1946). *Measuring business cycles*. New York: National Bureau of Economic Research.

Caraiani, P. (2010). Modeling business cycles in the Romanian economy using the Markov switching approach. *Romanian Journal of Economic Forecasting, 1*, 130–136.

Carrasco, M., Hu, L., & Ploberger, W. (2014). Optimal test for Markov switching parameters. *Econometrica, 82*, 765–784.

Chauvet, M. (1998). An econometric characterization of business cycle dynamics with factor structure and Markov switching. *International Economic Review, 39*, 969–996.

Chauvet, M., & Hamilton, J. (2006). Dating business cycle turning points. In C. Milas, P. Rotman, & D. Van Dijk (Eds.), *Nonlinear time series analysis of business cycles*. Amsterdam: Elsevier.

Cosslett, S. R., & Lee, L.-F. (1985). Serial correlation in discrete variable models. *Journal of Econometrics, 27*, 79–97.

Damette, O., & Rabah, Z. (2010). Datation du cycle Economique Français. *Revue française d'économie, 8*, 136–163.

Davies, R. B. (1977). Hypothesis testing when a nuisance parameter is present only under alternative. *Biometrika, 74*, 33–43.

Dempster, A. P., Laird, N. M., & Rubin, D. B. (1977). Maximum likelihood from incomplete data via the EM algorithm. *Journal of the Royal Statistical Society, B39*, 1–38.

Di Sanzo, S. (2009). Testing for linearity in Markov-switching models: A bootstrap approach. *Statistical Methods and Applications, 18*, 153–168.

Engle, R. F. (1982). Autoregressive conditional heteroscedasticity with estimates of the variance of U.K. inflation. *Econometrica, 50*, 987–1008.

Garcia, R. (1998). Asymptotic null distribution of the likelihood ratio test in Markov switching models. *International Economic Review, 39*, 763–788.

Gong, F., & Mariano, R. S. (1997). *Testing under non-standard conditions in frequency domain: with applications to Markov regime-switching models of exchange rates and federal funds rate*. New York: Federal Reserve Bank of New York (Staff Reports 23).

Goodwin, T. H. (1993). Business-cycle analysis with a Markov-switching model. *Journal of Business and Economic Statistics, 11*, 331–339.

Hamilton, J. D. (1989). A new approach to the economic analysis of nonstationary time series and the business cycle. *Econometrica, 57*, 357–384.

Hansen, B. E. (1992). The likelihood ratio test under non-standard conditions: Testing the Markov switching of GNP. *Journal of Applied Econometrics, 7*, S61–S82.

Harding, D., & Pagan, A. (2002). Dissecting the cycle: A methodological investigation. *Journal of Monetary Economics, 49*, 365–381.

Hendry, D. F. (1993). *Econometrics: Alchemy or science?*. Oxford: Blackwell Publishers.

Kaufmann, S. (2000). Measuring business cycles with a dynamic Markov switching factor model: An assessment using Bayesian simulation methods. *Econometrics Journal, 3*, 39–65.

Kim, C. J. (1994). Dynamic linear models with Markov switching. *Journal of Econometrics, 60*, 1–22.

Kim, C. J., & Nelson, C. R. (1999a). *State-space models with regime switching*. Cambridge, MA: MIT Press.

Kim, C. J., & Nelson, C. R. (1999b). Has the U.S. economy become more stable? A Bayesian approach based on a Markov-switching model of the business cycle. *Review of Economic and Statistics, 81*, 608–616.

Kontolemis, Z. G. (2001). Analysis of the US business cycle with a vector-Markov-switching model. *Journal of Forecasting, 20*, 47–61.

Krolzig, H.-M. (1997). *Markov switching vector autoregressions: Modelling, statistical inference and applications to business cycle analysis*. Berlin: Springer.

Laubscher, P. (2004). The SA business cycle over the 1990s and current prospects. *Journal for Studies in Economics and Econometrics, 28*, 21–43.

McConnell, M. M., & Perez-Quiros, G. P. (2000). Output fluctuations in the United States: What has changed since the early 1980s? *American Economic Review, 90*, 1464–1476.

Mintz, I. (1969). *Dating postwar business cycles: Methods and their applications to Western Germany, 1950–1967*. New York: National Bureau of Economic Research. Occasional Paper n°107.

Moolman, E. (2004). A Markov switching regime model of the South African business cycle. *Economic Modelling, 21*, 631–641.

Morley, J., & Rabah, Z. (2014). Testing for a Markov-switching mean in serially-correlated data. In M. Wohar & J. Ma (Eds.), *Recent advances in estimating nonlinear models*. Springer.

NBER (2010). *NBER business cycle dating committee*. Available on http://www.nber.org/cycles/recessions.html.

Perron, P., & Wada, T. (2009). Let's take a break: Trends and cycles in US real GDP. *Journal of Monetary Economics, 56*, 749–765.

Rabault, G. (1993). Une application du modèle de Hamilton. *Annales d'Economie et Statistique, 30*, 57–83.

Roux, A. (2011). *Everyone's guide to the South African economy* (10Th ed.). Cape Town: Zebra Press.

Teräsvirta, T. (2006). Forecasting economic variables with non-linear models. In G. Elliot, C. W. J. Granger, & A. Timmermann (Eds.), *Handbook of economic forecasting* (Vol. 1). Amsterdam: Elsevier.

Chapter 5
Forecasting

Abstract This chapter is devoted to the study of the German business cycle. In the tradition of Burns and Mitchell, it considers its classical form, which is represented by fluctuations in the series of the real Gross Domestic Product. After a methodological introduction, the chapter presents the main features of the German business cycle after dating it. Then it develops a probit model in order to predict recessions for the totality of the analyzed period. Finally, the chapter delivers a forecasting in real time for the most recent economic period.

Keywords Business cycles · Econometrics · Forecasting · Germany · Method ology · Probit models · Time series analysis

This chapter is devoted to the study of the German business cycle. More precisely, in the tradition of Burns and Mitchell, we consider its classical form, which is represented by fluctuations in the series of the real Gross Domestic Product (real GDP).

The following graph provides a stylized scheme of the cyclical movement for an imaginary economy. The recessions are temporal sequences where the real GDP in level decreases; inversely, the expansions are characterized by a growing real GDP. The passage from one phase to another is signaled by a turning point in the conjuncture: a *peak* (*trough*) is a highest (lowest) local turning point.

This chapter has received significant contributions from Reynald Majetti.

T. Aimar et al., *Business Cycles in the Run of History*,
SpringerBriefs in Economics, DOI 10.1007/978-3-319-24325-2_5

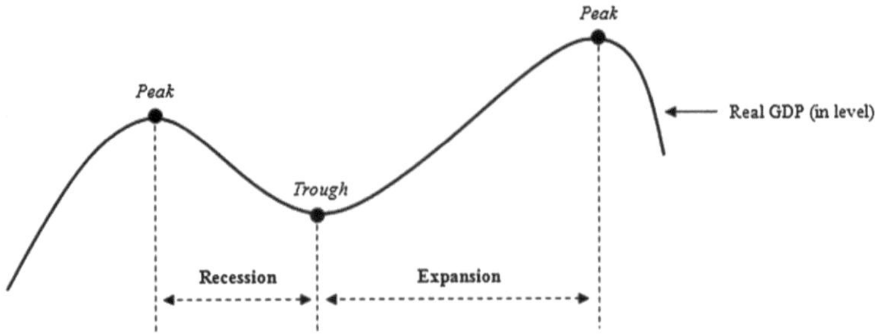

From the viewpoint of cyclical analysis, two questions are important: the identification and selection of turning points on one side; the forecasting of these points and thus, of the expansion and recession phases on other side.

Consequently, this chapter is organized in four sections. After this introduction, Sect. 5.2 studies the main features of the German business cycle after dating it. The Sect. 5.3 develops a probit model in order to predict recessions for the totality of the analyzed period. The last section delivers a forecasting in real time for the most recent economic period.

5.1 Chronology and Features of the German Cycle

Along this chapter, as we have specified it, interest is focused on the "classical business cycle" (CBC), defined as a succession of expansion and contraction phases.

5.1.1 BBQ Algorithm

CBC is gotten in searching the turning points of the real GDP series $y_t = \ln(Y_t)$. A *trough* is the analog of a local minimum and marks possibly the beginning (resp. the end) of an expansion (resp. a recession); a *peak* is the analog of a local maximum and signals the coming (resp. the end) recession (resp. of an expansion). Formally, for a given value of $K \in \mathbb{N}$, one can express a *turning point rule* as:

$$\begin{cases} peak\ at\ t = \{y_{t-k} < y_t > y_{t+k}\} \\ trough\ at\ t = \{y_{t-k} > y_t < y_{t+k}\} \end{cases}$$

with $k = 1, \ldots, K$.

More precisely, following Harding and Pagan (2002), we adapt the dating procedure associated with Bry and Boshan (1971, BB algorithm) to quarterly real

GDP. So we obtain the BBQ algorithm, for which the different stages of dating are summarized as follows:

1. Identifying a potential set of peaks and troughs using the *turning point rule* with K equal to 2 quarters;
2. Enforcing the condition that the peaks and troughs must alternate by selecting the highest (resp. lowest) consecutive peaks (resp. troughs);
3. Defining censoring rules.

The main rules aim to control the minimal duration of phases and cycles. Precisely, the business cycle phases must last a minimum of two quarters while a complete cycle—defined by the period of time between two peaks or two troughs—must be at least five quarters long. Complementary rules are finally designed to avoid false turning points:

- elimination of turns within two quarters of beginning and end of series;
- elimination of peaks (or troughs) at both ends of series which are lower (or higher) than values closer to end;
- elimination of phases for which the trough is higher than the peak.

The application of BBQ algorithm to real quarterly GDP allows us to establish a reference chronology of the German business cycle. Here is a table which gives the dates of peaks and troughs on the period 1970Q1–2014Q3.

The results in Table 5.1 indicate that the German economy has experienced 8 complete business cycles—from 'peak to peak' or from 'trough to trough'—since 1970. Their length varies from about 2 to 10.5 years for an average close to 5 years. (In comparison, the NBER's Business Cycle Dating Committee identifies for the US 6 cycles with an average length close to 6.5 years.) This chronology

Table 5.1 The German CBC

Peaks	Troughs	Duration of cycles (in quarters)	
		Trough from previous trough	Peak from previous peak
1974-Q1	1975-Q2	–	–
1980-Q1	1980-Q4	24	22
1982-Q1	1982-Q3	8	7
1992-Q1	1993-Q1	40	42
1995-Q3	1996-Q1	14	12
2001-Q2	2003-Q1	23	28
2004-Q2	2005-Q1	12	8
2008-Q1	2009-Q1	15	16
2012-Q3	2013-Q1	18	16
Mean		19.25	18.875

Note The dating chronology is based on the BBQ algorithm applied to the German real GDP series for the period 1970Q1–2014Q3

also exhibits the occurrence of 9 recessions (from 'peak to trough') and 8 expansions (from 'trough to peak'), for which it would be interesting to describe their characteristics.

5.1.2 Some Characteristics of the German Cycle

As pointed by Harding and Pagan (2002, p. 369), "Inspection of comments that are frequently made about the cycle suggests that there are four items of interest: the duration of the cycle and its phases, the amplitude of the cycle and its phases, any asymmetric behavior of its phases and cumulative movements within phases".

A convenient way to perceive these features is to represent a phase of a cycle as a triangle. For a particular phase i, its duration D_i and its amplitude A_i correspond to the base and the height of the triangle respectively. To sum up these two characteristics, an index of severity S_i is used to measure the area of the triangle:

$$S_i = 0.5 \times D_i \times A_i,$$

with $S_i > 0$ for an expansion phase and, $S_i < 0$ for a recession phase since the corresponding amplitude is negative. Figure 5.1 portrays the different possibilities for the so-called triangle.

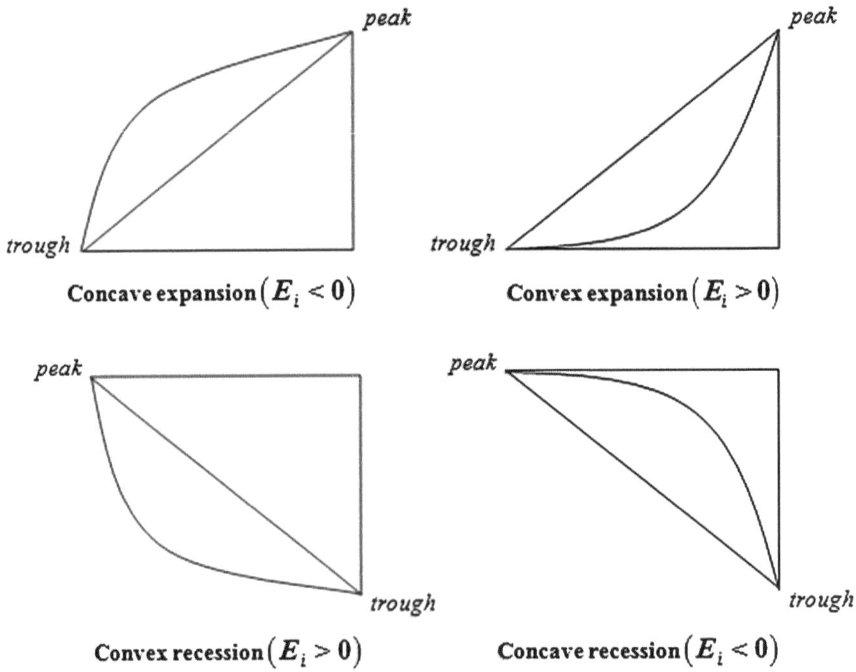

Fig. 5.1 The shape of business cycle phases

Note also that the measure S_i of the areas approximates the cumulated gains or losses through a phase and so it is referred to as *the triangle approximation to the cumulated movements*. In fact, the actual path through the phase may substantially differ from the linearity associated to the triangle approximation. So the difference between the actual C_i and approximated S_i cumulated movements leads to appreciate the departure from linearity and also the shape of the phase. To normalize this excess, Harding and Pagan (2002) have proposed the following index:

$$E_i = (S_i - C_i)/D_i.$$

Consequently, the sign of E_i points out to the fact that a particular phase may have a concave or a convex form (see Fig. 5.1). A positive excess index implies convexity meaning that the economic reversal is increasing through an expansion phase and decreasing in a recession phase. Conversely, concavity ($E_i < 0$) ensures that the cyclical reversals are high (low) in the beginning of an expansion (a recession) before declining (growing) as the phase extends. Finally, a null excess index would indicate a perfect linear path of cyclical fluctuations.

We compute this set of characteristics for the German cycle. The results are displayed in Table 5.2.

As previously highlighted, Germany suffered from 9 recessions since 1970. Among them, four occurred during the last fifteen years. Peculiarly valuable to

Table 5.2 Characteristics of the German CBC

Recessions				Expansions			
Period	Duration (quarters)	Amplitude (%)	Excess (%)	Period	Duration (quarters)	Amplitude (%)	Excess (%)
1974Q2–1975Q2	5	−2.43	−0.29	1975Q3–1980Q1	19	18.22	−0.57
1980Q2–1980Q4	3	−1.18	0.17	1981Q1–1982Q1	5	1.49	−0.29
1982Q2–1983Q3	2	−1.61	−0.09	1982Q4–1992Q1	38	31.10	2.36
1992Q2–1993Q1	4	−2.05	−0.04	1993Q2–1995Q3	10	4.97	0.12
1995Q4–1996Q1	2	−1.03	−0.23	1996Q2–2001Q2	21	12.02	0.04
2001Q3–2003Q1	7	−1.21	−0.40	2003Q2–2004Q2	5	1.25	0.02
2004Q3–2005Q1	3	−0.29	0	2005Q2–2008Q1	12	9.77	−0.17
2008Q2–2009Q1	4	−7.18	−1.84	2009Q2–2012Q3	14	8.80	−0.88
2012Q4–2013Q1	2	−0.82	0	2013Q2–	–	–	–
Mean	3.56	−1.98	−0.30	Mean	15.5	10.95	0.07

Source Authors' calculations

remark is the lowering of the GDP between 2001 and 2003: de facto, this corresponds to the longest downturn in the analyzed period, but its amplitude is relatively moderate with respect to others. The most severe contraction is undoubtedly that of 2008–2009 as the real GDP plunged by more than 7 % points. One can also emphasize the impact of the European sovereign debt crisis on the German economy as the latter indeed recorded two consecutive quarters of declining real GDP in 2012–2013.

Not surprisingly, the German CBC shows a high degree of asymmetry that takes various forms. First of all, the positive long-term trend inherent to the GDP series makes the expansions longer and ampler than recessions. The latter have an average duration of 3.6 quarters leading to an average decrease of 2 % points of real GDP, while the former last 15.5 quarters for a gain of 11 %. Moreover, the figures of excess reveal that the profile for the declining phase is concave in mean. This is especially true during the 'Great Recession': in parallel of the US economy and other developed countries, the German activity started by decreasing in early 2008 and then, this downswing was greatly accelerated with the intensification of the financial crisis in late 2008. On the contrary, the expansion periods do not tend to exhibit a unique profile.

5.2 The Econometric Model

We present the model used to analyze the German business cycle before to estimate it. Finally, we realize an in-sample prediction which is well-fitting to the dating of the turning points in the GDP series.

5.2.1 The Dynamic Probit

Consider the binary variable R_t, which takes value one in recessions and zero otherwise, and $\mathbf{x}_t$ a vector of $(k+1)$ explanatory variables, current or lagged, with $t = 1, \ldots, T$. In the static probit model, R_t is related to the regressors by

$$E(R_t|\mathbf{x}_t) = \Pr(R_t = 1|\mathbf{x}_t) = \Phi(\mathbf{x}_t'\boldsymbol{\gamma}) = \Phi(z_t), \tag{5.1}$$

where $E(.)$ denotes mathematical expectation and $\boldsymbol{\gamma}$ a vector of parameters. (Please note that the dimension of this vector is equal to $(k+1)$ since it includes a constant term.) Furthermore, $\Phi(\cdot)$ is the cumulative distribution function (CDF hereafter) of a standard normal variate.

To introduce the dynamic probit model, we define information set $I_t = \{R_t, \ldots, R_1, \mathbf{x}_t, \ldots, \mathbf{x}_1\}$. The dynamic analogue of (5.1) is then

$$E(R_t|I_{t-1}) = \Pr(R_t = 1|I_{t-1}) = \Phi(z_t), \tag{5.2}$$

where

$$z_t = \sum_{j=1}^{p} \rho_j R_{t-j} + \mathbf{x}'_{t-1}\boldsymbol{\gamma}. \tag{5.3}$$

The model defined by (5.2)–(5.3) is a simplified form of the Binary Autoregressive model, BARX(p), suggested by Zeger and Qaqish (1988). If we are not mistaken, the first economic paper to use a dynamic probit is that of Eichengreen et al. (1985). Thereafter, Dueker (1997), Chauvet and Potter (2005), Kauppi and Saikkonen (2008), Startz (2008), Ng (2012) and Bismans and Majetti (2013) have used the same model. (For a quick survey of the economic and econometric literature on the subject, see de Jong and Woutersen 2011.)

The estimation procedure of the static probit is well-known; that of its dynamic draft is more intricate, due to the presence of lagged values of the indicator R_t in the likelihood function.

Let $\boldsymbol{\beta} = (\rho_1, \ldots, \rho_p, \gamma_0, \gamma_1, \ldots, \gamma_k)$ denotes the true parameters of the probit model, $\boldsymbol{\rho} = (\rho_1, \ldots, \rho_p) \in \mathbb{R}^p$, $\boldsymbol{\gamma} = (\gamma_0, \gamma_1, \ldots, \gamma_k) \in \mathbb{R}^{k+1}$, $\mathbf{R}_{-p} = (R_{t-1}, \ldots, R_{t-p}) \in \mathbb{R}^p$. Moreover, $\mathbf{x}_{-1}$ is a $(k+1)$-dimensional vector of exogenous predictors.

Assuming the normality of perturbations, the log-likelihood function conditional on the first observations $R_1, \ldots, R_p$ is

$$\begin{aligned}\ln L(\hat{\boldsymbol{\beta}}_T) &= (T-p)^{-1} \sum_{t=p+1}^{T} \ln L_t(\hat{\boldsymbol{\beta}}) \\ &= (T-p)^{-1} \sum_{t=p+1}^{T} [R_t \ln(\Phi(\boldsymbol{\rho}'\mathbf{R}_{-p} + \boldsymbol{\gamma}'\mathbf{x}_{-1})) + (1-R_t)\ln(1-\Phi(\boldsymbol{\rho}'\mathbf{R}_{-p} + \boldsymbol{\gamma}'\mathbf{x}_{-1}))].\end{aligned} \tag{5.4}$$

The optimisation of the highly nonlinear log-likelihood function (5.4) can be carried out by standard numerical algorithms.

Furthermore, the estimated parameters present good asymptotical properties. de Jong and Woutersen (2011) prove that, given standard conditions, especially near epoch dependence of the random variables R_t, the maximum likelihood estimator $\hat{\boldsymbol{\beta}}_T$ is consistent so that $\hat{\boldsymbol{\beta}}_T \xrightarrow{P} \boldsymbol{\beta}$. Under another assumption, de Jong and Woutersen (2011, theorem 4) also prove that

$$T^{1/2}(\hat{\boldsymbol{\beta}}_T - \boldsymbol{\beta}) \xrightarrow{D} N(\mathbf{0}, \mathbf{I}^{-1}),$$

where $\mathbf{I}^{-1}$ is the inverse of the usual information matrix.

5.2.2 Empirical Model

As described in the previous section, the application of the BBQ algorithm to the German real GDP series allows us to determine the business cycle turning points and consequently, the chronology of recession and expansion periods. The corresponding variable of the model is *R* which takes the value one during the contractions and the value zero during the expansions.

As far as the choice for the lags of the binary variable, we follow the existent literature—e.g. Kauppi and Saikkonen (2008) or Bismans and Majetti (2013)—by introducing one lag only in the dynamic model. This is also justified by the business cycle's dating method insofar as a recession must last a minimum of two quarters. So, all things being equal, it is expected that the likelihood of a recession in the next quarter is much higher if the economy is already in a recession in the current quarter.

From there, our first task is to select the variables which must enter into the vector of predictors. Table 5.3 furnishes the list of these variables with their institutional source. Note that all the series cover the period 1973Q1–2013Q4.

Given that the EUR/USD exchange rate only exists since the beginning of the European Monetary System, the Eurostat institute has rebuilt a new series using particularly the European Currency Unit (ECU) for the period 1979–1999 and sooner.

The next task is now to select the optimal number of lags for each predictor. In this perspective, we use two measures for the predictive power of each variable: the pseudo R^2 developed by Estrella (1998) and the *t*-statistics computed with robust standard errors. The main results are reported in Table 5.4.

Several remarks can be drawn from the reading of this table. Firstly, except for the exchange rate EUR/USD, the coefficients are often highly and statistically different from zero. Secondly, the optimal number of lags is equal to 4 quarters for the SPREAD, to 1 quarter for the stock exchange indicator and to 3 quarters for the monetary aggregate. Thirdly, the predictive capacity of these variables selected at their optimum is appreciably the same with a R^2 close to 15 %. Consequently, we retain each of the three significant variables with its optimal lag to estimate the dynamic probit model.

Table 5.3 Statistical series

Series	Description	Source
SPI	Index of total share prices for all shares for Germany (quarterly growth rate)	OECD
SPREAD	Yield spread between 10-year German government bonds and 3-month EURIBOR	OECD
M1	Monetary Stock M1 (nominal aggregate for Eurozone) (semi-annual growth rate; seasonally adjusted)	ECB
ER	Spot exchange rate EUR/USD (1€ = x dollars)	Eurostat

Table 5.4 Pseudo R^2 and t-statistics

$x_{t\text{-}l}$	Model: $\Pr(R_t = 1 \mid x_{t-l}) = \Phi(\gamma_0 + \gamma_1 x_{t-l})$							
	l = lags (in quarters)							
	1	2	3	4	5	6	7	8
SPREAD	0.047 ***	0.090 ***	0.124 ***	**0.148** ***	0.114 ***	0.066 ***	0.026 **	0.007
ER	0.105 –	0.115 –	0.059 –	0.018 –	0.020 –	0.030 –	0.026 –	0.005 –
SPI	**0.139** ***	0.112 ***	0.073 ***	0.050 ***	0.045 ***	0.021 *	0.005	0
M1	0.023 **	0.095 ***	**0.15** ***	0.011 ***	0.048 ***	0.008	0.002	0.050

Note The table reports pseudo R^2 measures of fit for static probit models estimated over the entire sample period 1973Q1–2013Q4. Significance at the *10 %, **5 % and ***1 % levels is based on robust standard errors computed using the procedure of Newey and West (1987) (see also Kauppi and Saikkonen (2008) for technical details.)

5.2.3 *In-Sample Prediction*

In a first stage, given Eqs. (5.2)–(5.3) and the results in the previous subsection, the model to be estimated is the following:

$$\Pr(R_t = 1) = \Phi(\gamma_0 + \rho R_{t-1} + \gamma_1 SPREAD_{t-4} + \gamma_2 SPI_{t-1} + \gamma_3 M1_{t-3} + u_t),\quad t = 1, \ldots, T, \tag{5.5}$$

where $\Phi(\cdot)$ is the Gaussian CDF.

However, we must search the most parsimonious model. From then on, we proceed in three steps:

1. Estimation of the complete model with the three predictors: at this stage, it appears that the parameter associated with SPI is not significantly different from zero;
2. Estimation of the model with the two remaining predictors: all the coefficients are statistically significant;
3. Estimation of the model including the unique predictor M1; here also, the parameter is significant.

Finally, using the Bayesian Information Criterion (BIC) to compare the models estimated in the steps 2 and 3, we conclude that the last model is the better and thus must be selected. (This criterion takes the values 109.337 and 107.673 for the models 2 and 3 respectively; for more complete information on the reduction process and the transition among the models, see the Annex 1 to this chapter.)

The elimination of the SPREAD variable demands an explanation. It exists a large body of literature—see e.g. Harvey (1988, 1991, 1997), Estrella and Hardouvelis (1991), Estrella and Mishkin (1997, 1998), Dueker (1997), Dotsey (1998), Chauvet and Potter (2005), Moneta 2005, Nyholm (2007), Rosenberg and Maurer (2008), and also the survey by Wheelock and Wohar (2009)—which concludes to the predictive power of the rate spread. Nonetheless, in the present time where the short-term interest rate is near of zero, the correlation does not work. In these conditions, it is not surprising that the yield curve has a less predictive power than by the past.

Here are now the estimation results of the most parsimonious model including the only predictor M1.

Three principal observations can be formulated in reading Table 5.5. First, the coefficients for R and the monetary stock are significant at a level of 1 %; on the contrary, the constant of the dynamic probit is not significantly different from zero. Second, the coefficients of the two predictors have the expected sign: the lagged binary variable affects positively the probability of being in recession, while the latter is negatively related to the growth of the monetary aggregate M1. Third, the pseudo R^2 is near from 0.5, which is a good fitness for a qualitative model.

Applying the estimated model to the in-sample forecasting yields a scheme of German recessions. From this perspective, Fig. 5.2 shows the actual periods of recession such as they were determined by the BBQ algorithm, and the estimated probabilities of recession at each quarter for the time interval 1973Q1–2013Q4.

Some comments on the figure are welcome. One can firstly highlight that the warning signals correctly match the true periods of depression. Indeed, the recession probabilities are well synchronized with the business cycle turning points and they systemically reach a minimum of 60 % at the height of crisis. Moreover, there are no false signals outside, i.e. during the periods of expansion. Overall, we can conclude that our parsimonious model delivers a good in-sample performance in forecasting the German recessions since the 70s.

Table 5.5 In-sample estimation results

Variables	Coefficients	Error type
Constant	−0.383	0.424
R_{t-1}	1.913 ***	0.311
$M1_{t-3}$	−30.823 ***	10.968
Ln Likelihood = −46.187	Pseudo $R^2 = 0.455$	
RMSE = 0.2922	Bayesian information criterion = 107.673	

Note The dynamic probit model is estimated over the period 1973Q1–2013Q4. Significance at the *10 %, **5 % and ***1 % levels is based on robust standard errors

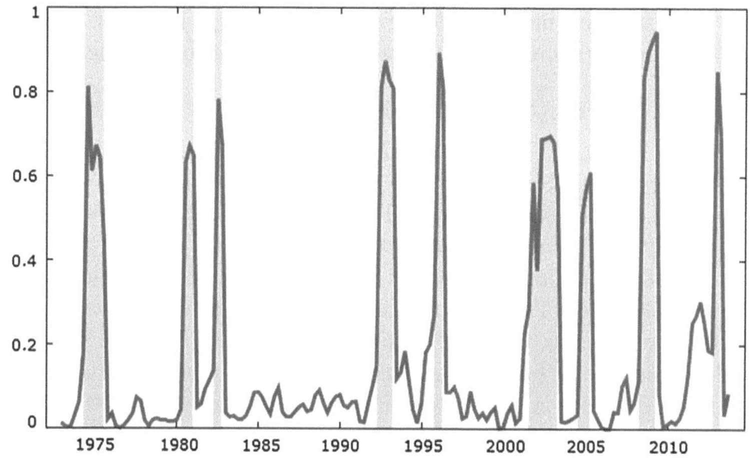

Fig. 5.2 In-sample forecasting. *Note* Recession probabilities are computed for the in-sample period 1973Q1–2013Q4. Shaded areas correspond to the recession phases identified with respect to the BBQ algorithm

5.3 Forecasting in Real Time

In the previous section, we have fundamentally realized a *retrospective* prediction of German recessions. To really assess the ability of our model to correctly anticipate business cycle turning points, we must now turn to an out-of-sample exercise in order to conduct a *prospective* analysis as regards the recession risk. Thus, we begin to develop the forecasting procedure before giving the predictions—in real time—with respect to the two last German recessions.

5.3.1 The Predicting Method

The problem we face is to predict a binary variable, denoted R_t, h quarters ahead given information at time $t - h$. It is well-known that the minimum mean-square error predictor of R_t based on information set I_{t-h} is given by

$$E(R_t|I_{t-h}),$$

i.e. by the conditional mean of R_t. As our model defined by (5.2) and (5.3) is truly dynamic, the conditional expectation of R_t, following the law of iterated expectations, becomes

$$E_{t-h}(R_t) = E_{t-h}\big[\Pr(R_t = 1|I_{t-1})\big], \tag{5.6}$$

where E_{t-h} denotes conditional mean with respect to I_{t-h}.

Using our estimated model with the lagged recession indicator and formula (5.3), optimal forecasting made at time $t - h$ thus requires to compute

$$\begin{aligned} E_{t-h}(R_t) &= E_{t-h}(\Phi(z_t)) \\ &= E_{t-h}\big(\Phi\left(\rho R_{t-1} + \mathbf{x}'_{t-l}\gamma\right)\big), \end{aligned} \tag{5.7}$$

where Φ is the CDF of a standard normal random variable, and $\mathbf{x}'_{t-l}$ is the row vector of the predictors with appropriate lags $l(l \geq h)$.

Prediction of R_t can be conducted in two manners: directly or iteratively (see Marcellino et al. 2006). The method used is a variant of this second procedure. Specifically, the forecasts have the particularity of being dynamic because they employ the chain rule of forecasting. This means that the probability of recession for a particular quarter t is generated using the prior forecast instead of using the true value—0 or 1—for the lagged binary indicator. In accordance with this recursive scheme, the general predictive formula (5.7) becomes

$$E_{t-h}(R_t) = \Phi\left(\rho \hat{R}_{t-1} + \mathbf{x}'_{t-l}\gamma\right), \tag{5.8}$$

with, $\hat{R}_{t-1} = E_{t-h-1}(R_{t-1})$ and $l \geq h$.

This procedure is especially useful in a real-time context where the true value of R_{t-1} may not be certain (or just unknown if the forecast horizon h is high). Indeed, the binary recession indicator relies on the GDP values, but the latter are known with a delay and are also subject to possible revisions over time that may alter the cyclical diagnosis. (In the Eurozone countries for example, the first GDP publication is done around 45 days after the end of the relevant quarter.) Thus, the recursive procedure makes it possible to avoid the problem related to R_{t-1} at the time the prediction is made, whatever the value for h.

By applying the law of iterations, one can also notice that the recursive forecasts given by (5.8) principally depend on the longer history of the variables included in $\mathbf{x}'_{t-l}$ and finally, we make the forecast horizon equal to the minimum value among the optimal lags l. In the next subsection, empirical analysis will be conducted through our most parsimonious model—the dynamic probit with the monetary aggregate M1—and thereby we could measure the likelihood of a recession up to 3 quarters ahead in real-time.

5.3.2 Forecasting the Recessions After 2005

The out-of-sample analysis leads us to distinguish the estimation period from the forecasting one. We choose to estimate the model over the restricted sample period 1973–2005. Beyond 2005, the true state of the economy is assumed unknown and we wish to evaluate in real time the recession risk using our most parsimonious model: the dynamic probit with the monetary aggregate M1.

Table 5.6 Out-of-sample forecasting procedure

Estimation	
Rolling window	1973Q1–2005Q4 → 1973Q1–2014Q3
Value of R_t after 2005	$R_t = \begin{cases} 1 \text{ if } \hat{R}_t \geq 0.5 \\ 0 \text{ if } \hat{R}_t < 0.5 \end{cases}$
Lag for R_t	$R_t = 0$
Prediction	
Fixed window	2006Q1–2015Q2
Recession probability	$E_{t-h}(R_t = 1) = \Phi\left(\gamma_0 + \rho\hat{R}_{t-1} + \gamma_1 M1_{t-3}\right)$, with, $\hat{R}_{t-1} = E_{t-h-1}(R_{t-1} = 1)$
Real-time horizon	$h = 3$

Taking into account the available data (up to 2014Q3) and the optimal lag ($l = 3$) for M1, the three-quarter-ahead forecasts are obtained from separate estimation samples running from 1973Q1–2005Q4 to 1973Q1–2014Q3. In this way, we are able to calculate the recession probabilities for the interval 2006Q1–2015Q2. To respect the real-time environment constraint, the rolling estimation will systemically use the last recession probability to re-estimate the model with one additional period. However, this implies to discretize the probability by using a threshold value between the two possible states of the economy and, in this regard, we naturally choose a threshold equal to 50 %. (To sum up the out-of-sample forecasting method, we provide Table 5.6.)

Figure 5.3 implements the out-of-sample method described supra. It reports the three-quarter-ahead predicted values for the probabilities and compares them with the realized values of the recession indicator across the interval 2006Q1–2015Q2.

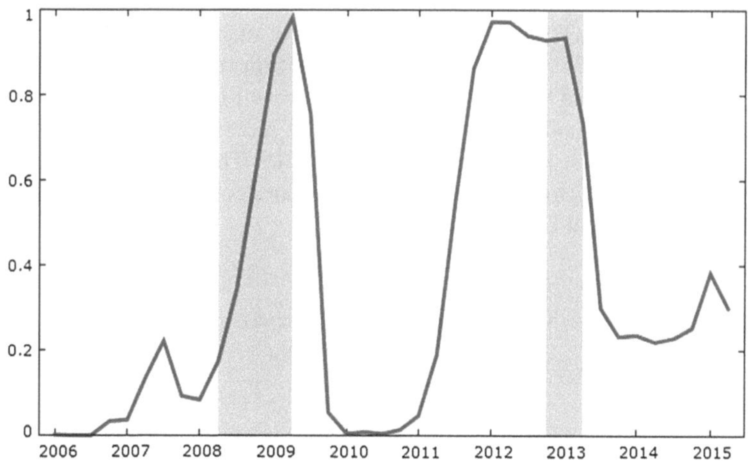

Fig. 5.3 Out-of-Sample forecasting. *Note* Recession probabilities are computed in real-time for the out-of-sample period 2006Q1–2015Q2. Shaded areas correspond to the recession phases identified with the BBQ algorithm

Indisputably, the dynamic probit model with M1 predicts quite well the 'Great Recession' of 2008–2009 and the European sovereign debt crisis leading to the last German recession in 2012–2013. However, beyond this general observation, two shades should be considered in order to better characterize the specific temporal path of German cyclical fluctuations:

1. The recession probabilities begin to increase in 2007 to reach 20 % in the middle of that year. These values remain relatively low until the beginning of 2008 and then they sharply increase during the second semester to reach more than 90 % at the height of the depression, i.e. in 2008Q4–2009Q1. From the middle of 2009, the warning signal falls very quickly until it completely disappears in 2010, a year during which the German real GDP grew by more than 4 %. However, as we can see on Fig. 5.3, our model does not deliver a perfectly synchronous signal with respect to the turning point reference dates.
2. As far as the second recession, it appears that the warning signal rises sharply during the year 2011—that is, when the sovereign debt crisis intensified in the euro area—and it remains close to a maximum (100 %) from 2012Q1 to 2013Q1. Clearly, the money supply still acts as a leading indicator of downturns in economic conditions, since the likelihood of a recession takes a value greater than 0.5 in the third quarter of 2011, i.e. a year before the German cycle had peaked. Note also that the model correctly predicts the ending date of the recession, given that the probability drops to 30 % from mid-2013.

If we now look at the period posterior to the last recession, we can draw an interesting observation. The probabilities never fall to zero, remaining slightly higher than 20 %, which indicates the absence of a true recovery. Table 5.7 allows us to compare the estimated probabilities with the quarterly growth rate of real GDP for Germany.

Clearly, one can see that the growth rate remains low after the end of the recession, except for 2013Q2 and 2014Q1. Moreover, it even becomes negative in the second quarter of 2014. These observed data confirm that the economic recovery has been very weak and thus that our forecasts are well-fitted to the reality.

Furthermore, our model yields a probability of recession equal to 38 and 30 % respectively in the first and second quarter of 2015. The conclusion to be drawn from this set of predictions is simple: the German economy is not immune to a recession in the current 2015!

Table 5.7 Real GDP growth (% change from previous quarter)

2013			2014		
Q2	Q3	Q4	Q1	Q2	Q3
0.8	0.3	0.4	0.8	−0.1	0.1

Source Eurostat

Annex 1: The Sequential Reduction Procedure

Variables	Models		
	(1)	(2)	(3)
Constant	−0.437 (0.425)	−0.384 (0.425)	−0.383 (0.424)
R_{t-1}	1.662*** (0.320)	1.783*** (0.318)	1.913*** (0.311)
$M1_{t-3}$	−23.315** (10.994)	−26.053** (0.264)	−30.823*** (10.968)
$SPREAD_{t-4}$	−0.170* (0.090)	−0.181** (0.092)	
SPI_{t-1}	−1.410 (1.156)		
ln *L*	−43.731	−44.469	−46.187
Pseudo R^2 (%)	45.545	44.637	42.527
Correct previsions (%)	89	89	89
Correct recessions (%)	65.6	62.5	68.75
RMSE	0.2807	0.2854	0.2922
BIC	112.961	109.337	107.673

References

Bismans, F., & Majetti, R. (2013). Forecasting recessions using financial variables. The French case. *Empirical Economics, 44*, 419–433.

Bry, G., & Boschan, C. (1971). *Cyclical analysis of time series: Selected procedures and computer programs*. New York: National Bureau of Economic Research, Technical Paper 20.

Chauvet, M., & Potter, S. (2005). Forecasting recessions using the yield curve. *Journal of Forecasting, 24*, 77–103.

De Jong, R. M., & Woutersen, T. M. (2011). Dynamic time series binary choice. *Econometric Theory, 27*, 673–702.

Dueker, M. J. (1997). Strengthening the case for the yield curve as a predictor of U.S. recessions. *Federal Reserve Bank of Saint Louis Review, 79*, 41–51.

Eichengreen, B., Watson, M., & Grossman, R. (1985). Bank rate policy under the interwar gold standard: A dynamic probit model. *Economic Journal, 95*, 725–745.

Estrella, A. (1998). A new measure of fit for equations with dichotomous dependent variables. *Journal of Business and Economic Statistics, 16*, 198–205.

Estrella, A., & Hardouvelis, G. (1991). The term structure as a predictor of real economic activity. *Journal of Finance, 46*, 555–576.

Estrella, A., & Mishkin, F. (1997). The predictive power of term structure on interest rates in Europe and United-States: Implication for the European Central Bank. *European Economic Review, 41*, 1375–1401.

Estrella, A., & Mishkin, F. (1998). Predicting U.S. recessions: Financial variables as leading indicators. *Review of Economics and Statistics, 80*, 45–61.

Harding, D., & Pagan, A. (2002). Dissecting the cycle: a methodological investigation. *Journal of Monetary Economics, 49*, 365–381.

Kauppi, H., & Saikkonen, P. (2008). Predicting U.S. recessions with dynamic binary response models. *Review of Economics and Statistics, 90*, 777–791.
Marcellino, M., Stock, J. H., & Watson, M. W. (2006). A comparison of direct and iterated multistep AR methods for forecasting macroeconomic series. *Journal of Econometrics, 135*, 499–526.
Moneta, F. (2005). Does the yield spread predict recessions in the Euro Area? *International Finance, 8*, 263–301.
Newey, W. K., & West, K. D. (1987). A simple, positive semi-definite, heteroskedasticity and autocorrelation consistent covariance matrix. *Econometrica, 55*, 703–708.
Ng, E. C. Y. (2012). Forecasting US recessions with various risk factors and dynamic models. *Journal of Macroeconomics, 34*, 112–125.
Nyholm, K. (2007). A new approach to predicting recessions. *Economic Notes, 36*, 27–42.
Rosenberg, J. V., & Maurer, S. (2008). Signal or noise? implications of the term premium for recession forecasting. *Federal Reserve Bank of New York Economic Policy Review, 12*, 1–11.
Startz, R. (2008). Binomial autoregressive moving average models with an application to U.S. recessions. *Journal of Business and Economic Statistics, 26*, 1–8.
Wheelock, D. C., & Wohar, M. E. (2009). Can the term spread predict output growth and recessions? a survey of the literature. *Federal Reserve Bank of Saint Louis Review, 91*, 419–440.
Zeger, S. L., & Qaqish, B. (1988). Markov regression models for time series: A quasi-likelihood approach. *Biometrics, 44*, 1019–1031.

Chapter 6
Afterword

Abstract This chapter begins with an examination and critical evaluation of the standard macroeconomic model. It continues by describing the core of the DSGE models and by showing the difficulties to explain the main features of the 2007–2008 global crisis. Finally, it gives a plea for mixing today macroeconomics and Hendry's econometric methodology.

Keywords 2007–2008 crisis · DSGE models · Hendry's methodology · Macroeconomics · Real Business Cycle (RBC) theory

6.1 A Plea for a New Econometrics-Based Macroeconomics

This book has first outlined the theories of the business cycles since the Industrial Revolution before to develop modern approaches of the economic fluctuations. The emprical chapters are devoted respectively to the dating and forecasting of the upturns and downturns of global activity, that is to say, in brief, to date and predict the recessions.

Following Popper's epistemology and referring to the criterion of falsifiability, then clearly, the approach used is appropriate: it makes it possible, on the German example, to forecast correctly and in real time, the last two recessions. A flat must still be introduced, as the predictive model is not based on a strictly determined theory.

However, it is a largely shared and popular opinion that the economic theory, thus macroeconomics, has failed to predict and explain the occurrence of the 2008–2009 global crisis. At a more scientific level, such a proposition must be refined: the Standard Model, defined in the seminal paper of Kydland and Prescott (1982) and developed after by many authors, really proved to be a poor

T. Aimar et al., *Business Cycles in the Run of History*,
SpringerBriefs in Economics, DOI 10.1007/978-3-319-24325-2_6

explanatory tool for understanding the burst of the American housing bubble and more generally the Great Recession.

6.2 The Standard Macroeconomic Model

In reality, the initial Real Business Cycle (RBC) theory has become, under the form of Dynamic Stochastic General Equilibrium (DGSE) models, the core of the current macroeconomics. Certainly, there exist many variants of this canonical structure, mainly classical and new Keynesian ones. However, the existence of a reference framework common to these big variants is out-of doubt (see, for example, the sentence of Gali (2008, p. 4), a leading New Keynesian, on the similarities between the two approaches).

The principal features of the DSGE core model such as described by Gali (2008) and Wickens (2008, Chap. 14) are the following:

- Above all, the standard theory considers that the macroeconomic relations must be based on solid microfoundations, what implies using a representative consumer and firm;
- The representative household maximizes, under budget constraint, an intertemporal utility function, whose the arguments are the future consumptions and often the hours of labour (employment if preferred):

$$E_t \sum_{s=0}^{+\infty} \beta^s U(C_{t+s}, H_{t+s}),$$

where C denotes the consumption (a composite good), H the working hours and β is a discount factor.
- The firm is provided with a Cobb-Douglas function with constant returns to scale and two production factors, capital and labour. The production function is also driven by technological change operating under the scheme:

$$y_t = A_t K_t^{\alpha} N_t^{1-\alpha}.$$

The A parameter evolves exogenously according to a stochastic process, generally a random walk with drift:

$$\Delta A_t = \mu + \varepsilon_t, \quad \varepsilon_t \sim I.I.D(0, \sigma^2),$$

where μ denotes the long run rate of variation of technological change and ε_t a non-autocorrelated productivity shock.
- Conditions of first order for firm and consumer are substituted to the usual behavioral equations of the macroeconomics. The equilibrium is reached when the output is equal to the sum of consumption and investment; *in fine*, the equilibrium levels of output and employment are functions of technology, whilst the

productivity shocks generate correlated movements of the aggregate variables in the economy: production, capital, investment, consumption and employment.
- Finally, I retain two additional characteristics of the core model, namely the using of rational expectations hypothesis and especially the fact that it is calibrated, not statistically estimated.

Evidently, at any time, markets are supposed to be in a general equilibrium state, where the supply equates the demand. The representative consumer and firm act in an environment of perfect competition. The policy prescription results logically from this analysis: don't react to the fluctuations in the economy; cycles are simply equilibrium cycles, unemployment is voluntary. There is no place for Keynesian unemployment. As the title of the Grant (2014)'s book says it, depression cures itself!

With respect to this core framework, the new Keynesian brand includes non-classical peculiarities such as monopolistic competition, nominal rigidities with sticky prices and also, short run non-neutrality of monetary policy.

6.3 A Critical Evaluation

Flaws or shortcomings of the Standard Model are numerous. From my viewpoint, the main are of two orders: the assumption of representative agents and that of the existence of a system of complete markets. (I leave aside the question of the rational expectations hypothesis (REH), because it assumes too strong cognitive capacities from the economic agents as pointed, for example, by De Grauwe (2010); the environment of these agents indeed is extraordinarily complex.) However, before to examine it, some remarks on General Equilibrium Theory (GET) are in point. In the sixties, GET seemed to have reached a level of generality and formalization, which made it close to completion. Theory—the Arrow-Debreu model—had demonstrated the existence of at least one general equilibrium for a competitive economy and its equivalence with an optimum of Pareto. In addition, it had also operated the synthesis with the theory of cooperative games via the concept of core.

However, in the next decade, the theory enters into a deep crisis due to unexpected results. On one side, Sonnenschein (1972), Debreu (1974) and Mantel (1974)—these papers are very technical; for an easier presentation, see Kirman (1992)—proofed almost simultaneously, but independently, that the excess demand functions (demand minus supply) were completely characterized by three properties: the Walras law, the continuity and homogeneity. In other words, given usual hypotheses on the preferences, initial resources and consumer utility function, nothing could be said about the form of aggregate demand function; peculiarly, it is impossible to prove that this function has a negative slope. On another side, in the seventies, several papers by Akerlof, Spence and especially, Rotschild and Stiglitz (1976) have demonstrated that information asymmetries could not integrated adequately in the Arrow-Debreu model. Consequently, the "good" properties of efficiency, optimality, etc., of the model are not preserved in presence of such asymmetries. Moreover, in this occurrence, markets may be in disequilibrium.

Stiglitz (2011, p. 596) has correctly pointed the paradox that new classical macroeconomics had adopted the Arrow-Debreu model, even though its foundations "were just being undermined by advances in the economics of information and game theory". I add: also by the "impossibility theorem" of Sonnenschein, Debreu and Mantel. This has an important implication: it constraints RBC theory to use the fiction of a representative consumer or firm, because there are no possibility to aggregate the individual behaviours from a theoretical viewpoint. Yet in our economies, there is, for example, glaring examples of income inequalities between individuals.

As far as the story of complete markets is concerned, the implications of the adoption of the GE model by the RBC theorists are also important. In his beautiful monograph, Debreu (1959, Chap. 7) following Arrow has extended the theory to uncertainty. Formally, a commodity is now defined by its physical properties, its location, its date, but also by an event which the realization conditions the delivery of the commodity. So we get contingent goods and prices. Nevertheless, the existence of one (at least) general equilibrium for this uncertain economy and the results relating in terms of efficiency are conditional on the parallel existence of a complete markets system, one for each contingent commodity. In the real world, there are much less contingent markets or future than what the theory requires. In this sense, the reality is that of incomplete markets. The problem is then that most efficiency results become obsolete (for a way to go out this contradiction, see Magill and Quinzii (1996)).

This critical evaluation focuses on the Standard Model, where the effects of technological shocks on the real aggregate variables are studied. However, many successive stones have been added to the basic RBC structure such as open economies, fiscal and monetary shocks and son one.

If the money is introduced into the model, a problematic result is gotten: the dynamic path of the previous real variables is not affected by the monetary policy, what means that this one is neutral against of these variables. Furthermore, in this perspective, it's important to note the money is only conceived as a unit of account, a Walrasian *numéraire* for all the prices throughout the economy. Its other functions—store of values, medium of exchanges—are neglected.

And now look at the mode by which the core model is made operational. RBC theorists use a technique called "calibration". Peculiarly, Kydland and Prescott (1991) proposed a four-step procedure, curiously named "econometrics of general equilibrium". These four stages are the following: define interest situation or question; set up the model; calibrate this model and realize some "computational experiments", and finally report the findings and results. Applying this procedure to the measure of business cycles fluctuations yields the conclusion that "the model economy's output variance is 55 % as large as the corresponding variance for the US economy in the postwar period."

The calibrating approach is highly controversial. Here it will suffice to say that encryption of the model parameters is not based upon the techniques of statistical inference and thus the overall procedure is basically flawed (there exist more recent methods of optimal calibration using usual statistical techniques developed by econometricians; one of these is the indirect inference: see for example Gouriéroux and Monfort (1996), and also Dejong with Dave (2007, 2011)).

6.4 The Turmoil of the 2007–2008 Crisis

The influence of RBC approach to the business cycles has been limited to the academic circus. The same thing could not say for new Keynesian dynamic stochastic general equilibrium (DSGE) models. The latter were largely the product of a cooperation between academia and central banks of developed countries. (For example, European central banks fund thc Euro Area Business Cycle Network to sustain research in the domain of economic cycle.)

In this strand, one of the first among these specific DSGE models is that of Smets and Wouters (2003). It retains the main features of the core structure—intertemporal optimization for households, one final composite good produced on a perfectly competitive market, etc. However, the utility function of households—in fact, there is a continuum of consumers—depends now of consumption relative to a habit variable, of worked hours, and of real-money balances. The model also incorporates some decisive new Keynesian characteristics, in particular, sticky prices and wages, and a continuum of monopolistically produced intermediate goods. Two other features are valuable to be quoted: on one side, ten stochastic shocks are introduced into the model (five shocks arising from technology and preferences; three cost-push shocks and two monetary shocks); on the other side, the model is estimated using Bayesian techniques, particularly by minimizing the posterior distribution of the parameters.

Now, the follow stage is to confront models and reality. Looking at the unfolding of the economic and financial crisis of 2007–2009 allows to isolate some stylized facts especially important for analysis—see in particular Shiller (2008) and Turner (2012):

- Making of a housing bubble between 2000 and 2007 which generated the subprime crisis;
- Emergence of serious tensions since August 2007 on money markets with soaring of risk premia;
- Generalized credit boom accompanied by increasing profits or returns boosted by leverage;
- Development of a shadow banking system;
- Big run on key funding markets after the default of Lehman Brothers;
- Impossibility to attribute a price to Asset-backed Securities and Structured CDO's;

- The unmatched depth of the recession begun in December 2007 in the United States and in the second quarter of 2008 for the main European countries;
- Growing gap between the size of financial institutions balance sheets and that of real branches of the economies, but also in the distribution of revenues;
- Etc.

It was enough to make a list of these characteristics to realize that none of them is considered by DSGE models. The reason is that these do not incorporate financial intermediation or a sector of credit. As far as the depth of recession is concerned, the line of defence consists of saying that the paradigm "is clearly applicable to normal times" (Gali, 2009, p. 3). Conclusion: the modelling ignores deep depressions, which is precisely the object to study and analyse.

The twin crises—financial and economic—have triggered a big movement of adaptation and revision of the DSGE models. On the side of new classics, some authors tried to give an explicative scheme of the 2008–2009 recession—a good example is furnished by Ohanian (2010) and by Hall (2010). The new-Keynesian network is working to a fresh generation of DSGE models, including financial intermediation and the policies to reach and preserve the financial stability—see the three examples presented in Neri (2012).

Obviously, policy-makers does not wait; solving structural problems either. It is perhaps possible that in the future, DSGE models will provide answers to policy issues really important. Clearly, it is not the case today. Consequently, I agree on the objective defined by Stiglitz (2011, p. 636): building a New Macroeconomics which "incorporates an analysis of risk, information, and institutions set in a context of inequality, globalisation, and structural transformation (…)" In this perspective of reconstruction, econometrics is called to play a major role.

6.5 Macroeconomics Otherwise

Almost since the economics has acted as a scientific discipline, a strong struggle has developed about the question of relations between theories and facts. Without going back in the past, it will suffice to recall the controversy opposing Burns and Mitchell at one side, and Koopmans (1947) on the other, the latter accusing the former to make "measurement without theory". In the last decades, the econometrics has experimented the same opposition. At one pole is found the RBC calibrators focused on structural parameters—I have shown it above—, for who the only problem is to match theory-driven models to data; at the other, Sims (1980a, b) criticizes macroeconometric modelers and their propensity to introduce many identification restrictions, in fact, totally "incredible", but induced from a theoretical viewpoint. At the opposite, Sims proponed to use vector autoregressions (VAR) instead macromodels. (In VAR systems, each variable is regressed on its own past and the lags of all the other variables within the system. Thereafter have been implemented structural VAR's.) As soon as one rejects the opposition theory-driven methodology versus data-driven, what then is the proper epistemological position?

Indeed, the question regarding the relations between theoretical analysis and empirics has been strongly debated in all the areas of sciences and also in philosophy. Popper (1989, p. 46 and sq.) has developed an acute critic of the proposition that "science proceeds from observations to theory". For him, this way is nothing other than a belief. Moreover, he gave a solution to the called "induction problem" However, the Popperian criticism does not justify the contrary view, which pushes unilaterally the accent on the theory notwithstanding the reality. In fact, the true question is how to link theories and data so that the process of knowledge is scientific from side to side. In terms of Popper, "How do we jump from an observation statement to a good theory?" In econometrics, the interrogation should be formulated as following: "How do we jump from a set of statistical series to good empirical models?"

This difficult, albeit fundamental problem has been the subject of major methodological debates among econometricians (a good overview of the different positions expressed is given in Granger (1990)). From my viewpoint, it is David Hendry's econometric methodology, which represents the best response to the question. Therefore, I will now synthetize the salient points of his analysis (I will use Hendry (1990, 2009), and mainly, Hendry and Doornik (2014); see also, the older contribution of Gilbert (1986)).

First, we consider a society at a given instant. This society is plugged-in history. Furthermore, each of its building elements is intertwined with the other. However, we are especially interested by the trends at work in the economic sphere, but I would be a methodological error to neglect the relevant variables from other spheres of the social formation under study. Consequently, the starting point of the knowledge process is made by the Global Data Generation Process (GDGP); itself reduced to the Local Data-Generating Process (LDGP) by taking account exclusively the variables interconnected from the angle adopted in the analysis. Even reduced, the LDGP is a highly multidimensional joint probability distribution associated with a huge vector of variables—in our case, time series. The problem is after to implement General-to-specific (GETS) methodology to approximate the LDGP and finally to select a good explaining model of the phenomenon under review. (Gets is the acronym created by Hendry and PcGets was the first denomination of a software developed by Doornik and Hendry.)

The starting point of the Gets methodology consists of the formulation of a General Unrestricted Model (GUM). Economic theories are used to suggest a preliminary specification of the GUM. The model must then undergo several operations of "reduction" before providing a satisfactory picture of the analysed relations.

In total, the procedure formally involves three main steps. The first stage is theory-based; it consists to specify a relationship between the interest variable y and a set of explanatory variables represented by the vector of dimension K denoted $\mathbf{x}$:

$$y_t = f_t(\mathbf{x}), \quad t = 1, \ldots, T.$$

All the problem at this stage is to select the K variables defining the LDGP in the light of economic theories, but also of institutional elements and historical events.

The next step is characterized by embedding the vector $\mathbf{x}$ in a more general framework with lags on the components of $\mathbf{x}$ and non-linear terms $g(\cdot)$. Assume that r is the longest lag on the set of K variables x and denote by $\mathbf{1}_{i=t}$ a list of T indicators introduced to take account structural breaks and outliers in the data. The GUM then can be written as

$$y_t = \sum_{j=1}^{r} \beta'_j \mathbf{x}_{t-j} + \sum_{j=1}^{r} \gamma'_j \mathbf{g}(\mathbf{x}_{t-j}) + \sum_{j=1}^{r} \alpha_j y_{t-j} + \sum_{i=1}^{T} \delta_i \mathbf{1}_{i=t} + \varepsilon_t.$$

In the third step, the task is to reduce the previous GUM so that by collecting the selected indicators in a vector $\boldsymbol{d}$ yields the final specific and simple specification:

$$y_t = \sum_{k=1}^{r^*} \alpha_k y_{t-k} + \sum_{k=0}^{r^*} \boldsymbol{\beta}_k^{*\prime} \mathbf{x}_{t-k}^{*} + \sum_{k=0}^{r^*} \boldsymbol{\gamma}_k^{*\prime} \mathbf{g}(\mathbf{x}_{t-k}^{*}) + \boldsymbol{\xi}' \mathbf{d}_t + \nu_t,$$

where ν_t is an innovation process. This stage of the procedure is evidently crucial. It includes especially the twin operations of reductions: marginalisation by conditioning of the GDGP and sequential factorization herein. Note that this step also requires that the conditioning variables are weakly exogenous for the interest parameters, what allows valid inferences from the conditional distribution, equivalent to inferences from the joint distribution (the classical paper on exogeneity is that of Engle et al. (1982); Engle (1984) has designed a test for weak exogeneity). So a parsimonious, congruent, i.e. coordinated to the real, model is finally gotten, product through the application of the General-to-specific methodology.

Now some words on prediction are in point, because the test of all theory is its predictive capacity. In their diversity, forecasting methods try to extrapolate present and past information into the future. However, future can know structural breaks or location shifts, which entail serious errors in forecasts. The problem is even more acute as economic series are mostly non-stationary. The solution is then to search for an appropriate predictive model by imposing on LDGP specification some transformations that will avoid systematic forecasting errors. It is the procedure implemented successfully in the Chap. 4 of this book.

The path to rebuild macroeconomics with solid econometric foundations is still long, but by following this path, reliable results in terms of explanation and prediction are available immediately or will become it quickly. In other words, it is promising way.

The yards are open!

Francis Bismans

References

De Grauwe, P. (2010). The scientific foundation of dynamic stochastic general equilibrium (DSGE) models. *Public Choice, 144*, 413–443.

De Jong, D. N., & Dave, C. (2007). *Structural macroeconometrics*. Princeton, Oxford: Princeton University Press.

De Jong, R. M., & Woutersen, T. M. (2011). Dynamic time series binary choice. *Econometric Theory, 27*, 673–702.

Debreu, G. (1959). *Theory of value. An axiomatic analysis of economic equilibrium*. New York, London: Wiley.

Debreu, G. (1974). Excess demand functions. *Journal of Mathematical Economics, 1*, 15–21.

Engle, R. F. (1982). Autoregressive conditional heteroscedasticity with estimates of the variance of U.K. inflation. *Econometrica, 50*, 987–1008.

Engle, R. F. (1984). Wald, likelihood ratio, and lagrange multiplier tests in econometrics. In Z. Griliches & M. D. Intriligator (Eds.), *Handbook of econometrics* (Vol. II, pp. 775–826) Amsterdam, New York, Oxford: North-Holland Publishing Company.

Gali, J. (2008). *Monetary policy, inflation, and the business cycle. An introduction to the New Keynesian framework*. Princeton-Oxford: Princeton University Press.

Gali, J. (2009). *Interview with Andrew Scott (former Scientific Chair of the EABCN)*. At http://www.eabcn.org/sites/all/files/Andrew_Scott_and_Jordi_Gali_final_0.pdf.

Gilbert, C. L. (1986). Professor Hendry's econometric methodology. *Oxford Bulletin of Economics and Statistics, 48*, 283–307. Reprinted in Granger (1990).

Gouriéroux, C., & Monfort, A. (1996). *Simulation-based econometric methods*. Oxford, New York: Oxford University Press.

Granger, C. W. J. (Ed.). (1990). *Modelling economic series. Readings in econometric methodology*. Oxford: Clarendon Press.

Grant, J. (2014). *The forgotten depression. 1921: The crash that cured itself.* New York: Simon & Schuster.

Hall, R. E. (2010). Why does the economy fall to pieces after a financial crisis. *Journal of Economic Perspectives, 24*, 3–20.

Hendry, D. F. (1990). Econometrics—Alchemy or Science? *Economica, 47*, 387–406. Reprinted in Hendry, D. F. (2000). *Econometrics: Alchemy or science? Essays in econometric methodology*, new edition, Oxford, New York: Oxford University Press.

Hendry, D. F. (2009). The Methodology of empirical econometric modeling: Applied econometrics through the looking-glass. In T. C. Mills & K. D Patterson (Eds.), *Palgrave handbook of econometrics. Applied econometrics* (Vol. 2, pp. 3–67). Basingstoke: Palgrave MacMillan.

Hendry, D., & Doornik, J. A. (2014). *Empirical model discovery and theory evaluation. Automatic selection methods in econometrics*. Cambridge, London: MIT Press.

Kirman, A. (1992). Whom and what does the representative individual represent? *Journal of Economic Perspectives, 6*, 117–136.

Koopmans, T. C. (1947). Measurement without theory. *Review of Economics and Statistics, 29*, 161–179.

Kydland, F., & Prescott, E. (1982). Time to build and aggregate fluctuations. *Econometrica, 50*(1982), 1345–1370.

Kydland, F., & Prescott, E. (1991). The econometrics of the general equilibrium approach to business cycles. *Scandinavian Journal of Economics, 93*, 161–178. Reprinted in Hylleberg, S., & Paldam, M. (Eds.), *New approaches to empirical macroeconomics*. Oxford, Cambridge: Blackwell Publishers.

Magill, M., & Quinzii, M. (1996). *Theory of incomplete markets*. Cambridge, London: MIT Press.

Mantel, R. R. (1974). On the characterization of aggregate excess demand. *Journal of Economic Theory, 7*, 348–353.

Neri, S. (2012). *Financial intermediation and the real economy: What role monetary and macro-prudential policies?* Prepared for the SUERF\Deutsche Bundesbank/IMFS Conference "The ESRB at 1", Berlin, November 8–9, 2011.

Ohanian, L. E. (2010). The economic crisis from a neoclassical perspective. *Journal of Economic Perspectives, 24*, 45–66.

Popper, K. (1989). *Conjectures and refutations. The growth of scientific knowledge* (fifth edition ed.). London, New York: Routledge.

Rotschild, M., & Stiglitz, J. E. (1976). Equilibrium in competitive insurance markets: An essay on the economics of imperfect information. *Quarterly Journal of Economics, 90*, 629–649.

Shiller, R. J. (2008). *The subprime solution. How today's global financial crisis happened, and what to do about it*. Princeton, Oxford: Princeton University Press.

Sims, C. (1980a). Macroeconomics and reality. *Econometrica, 48*, 1–48.

Sims, C. (1980b). Comparison of interwar and postwar cycles: monetarism reconsidered. *American Economic Review, 70*, 250–257.

Smets, F., & Wouters, R. (2003). An estimated dynamic stochastic general equilibrium model of the Euro area. *Journal of the European Economic Association, 1*, 1123–1175.

Sonnenschein, H. (1972). Market excess demand functions. *Econometrica, 40*, 543–549.

Stiglitz, J. E. (2011). Rethinking macroeconomics: What failed, and how to repair it. *Journal of the European Economic Association, 9*, 591–645.

Turner, A. (2012). *Economics after the crisis. Objectives and means*. Cambridge, London: MIT Press.

Wickens, M. (2008). *Macroeconomic theory. A dynamic general equilibrium approach*. Princeton, London: Princeton University Press.

MIX
Papier aus verantwortungsvollen Quellen
Paper from responsible sources
FSC® C105338

If you have any concerns about our products,
you can contact us on
ProductSafety@springernature.com

In case Publisher is established outside the EU,
the EU authorized representative is:
Springer Nature Customer Service Center GmbH
Europaplatz 3, 69115 Heidelberg, Germany

Printed by Libri Plureos GmbH
in Hamburg, Germany